No More Leftovers

By Bishop Dennis Leonard

No More Leftovers

By Bishop Dennis Leonard

CONTENTS

Dedication		I
Introduction		II
1	NO MORE LEFTOVERS	1
2	OVERCOMING THE SPIRIT OF FAILURE	15
3	OVERCOMING FAILURE IN RELATIONSHIPS	28
4	DEALING WITH YOUR ANGRY SELF	48
5	COURAGE UNDER FIRE	64
6	WALKING ON EGGSHELLS	78
7	OVERCOMING FAILURE THROUGH PRAYER	92
8	REVERSE THE CURSE	106
9	DESTINY DECISIONS	122
10	THE GREAT PRETENDER	140
11	TRUTH OR CONSEQUENCES	150
12	I AM NOT THE JUDGE	166
13	I WILL NOT BE A FAILURE FOREVER	180
14	THE POWER OF YOUR WORDS	198
15	LET IT GO	214
16	CONCLUSION - OVERCOMING THE GUILT OF MY PAST	230
	ABOUT THE AUTHOR	246

DEDICATION

I dedicate this book to the people who have had nothing but "leftovers" their entire life. I believe that your faith will be increased and you'll see that God wants to bless you. I trust that you'll see that leftovers are not for the child of God, and He wants you to be blessed. It's time to believe for your turn around today. It's time to believe that your best days are still ahead.In other words, if we will put God first in every area of our lives, God says we will be the head and not the tail. If we will put Him first in every part of our lives, God says "no good thing will He withhold from those who will walk upright before Him."

I

XII

INTRODUCTION

Anytime we struggle to get on our feet, we are grateful for any help that comes our way. Anytime we struggle trying to make a living, we are grateful for hand me downs that are given to us. Anytime we struggle to buy food for our families we are grateful for any leftovers that come our way. But when we find out who we are in Christ, we find out that God never made us for hand me downs and leftovers. In fact, God said if we are willing and obedient we will eat the good or best of the land.

Since God delights in the prosperity of those who love and serve Him, I can believe God to help me financially in my life. Since God wants me to prosper and be in health as my soul prospers, then I can believe God to own my own house. I can

II

believe God to be a property owner.

As you read this book, I want to you to start using your faith to be blessed. I want you to believe in your heart that if you are willing and obedient in every part of your life, that God will bless you beyond your wildest dreams. I want you to believe that He will do exceedingly abundantly beyond all you can ask or think. Even if you're accustomed to hand me downs and leftovers, you need to know that God has a lot of goodness stored up for anyone that will serve Him with their whole hearts. God has a lot of mercy stored up for anyone that is willing and obedient.

If you are going to fulfill your destiny, you can't live your life any old way. If you're tired of living under a spirit of failure, it's time to let go of the past and make some plans for the future. It's time to serve an eviction notice on the devil and tell him you're through with that grasshopper mentality. It's time to be like Joshua and step into our Promised Land. If we don't turn to the left or the right, we will see success in our lives. If we will be strong in the Lord and the power of His might, we will make our way prosperous. If we will do things God's way, we can see things turn around very quickly and be through with leftovers once and for all.

When we look at scripture, we can see that God's people were always out numbered. But when they put God first in every part of their lives, He always caused them to win. That's why I'm changing some things in my life today. I've decided to do things God's way and I'm ready to be blessed. Yes, I've made a lot of mistakes in the past. Yes, I've had a lot of failures in my life. But that was then and this is now. I can't change where I've been, but I can change where I'm going. I'm putting God first in every part of my life, and God will cause me to be victorious. "Many are the afflictions of the righteous, but the Lord shall deliver me out of them all."

I've made up my mind to trust God in a new way. I'm putting the Lord first, and it's only a matter of time until He brings me out of my trouble. I am willing and obedient and in due season, God will bring my breakthrough. I am diligently obeying Him and He's continually blessing me.

1

No More Leftovers

There is a time in all of our lives that we are grateful to God for hand-me-downs and leftovers. But as we grow up in Christ, there is a time to believe God for the best. No good thing will He withhold from those who walk upright before Him. (Psalm 84:11)

If you come from an abusive past, then you probably struggle with low self-worth. If you come from an abusive relationship, then you are probably challenged with negative thinking. You may even think that you're not good enough or that you can't accomplish certain things. But you have to know, when you gave your life to the Lord Jesus Christ, everything began to change. God wants His children to be blessed.

The enemy's plan is for you to be so beaten down in life that you think you are not worth much. His plan is to discourage you and make you to think that you can never accomplish anything. His plan is to make you believe that you'll never own your own house. His plan is to make you think that you'll have nothing but leftovers all of your life.

> *If ye be willing and obedient, ye shall eat the good of the land...*
> *Isaiah 1:19*

The Bible says, "As a man thinketh in his heart, so is he" (Proverbs 23:7). In other words, if you don't think much of yourself, then no one else will either. If you think you are nothing but a failure, then you will likely become a failure. Make no mistake, our spiritual enemy wants us to think that we are nothing but grasshoppers and failures. That's his plan! He wants us to think that we are too unworthy. Let me tell you something, we are all unworthy. It's the Blood of Jesus covering our lives that makes us worthy.

Your spiritual enemy wants you to think that God can never use somebody like you. He wants you to believe that you are no good so that you won't use your faith in God. He wants you to think that you are the one who has committed the unpardonable sin. But let me tell you, the only unpardonable sin is rejecting Jesus Christ as Lord and Savior of your life.

The enemy wants you to think that there is no use in trying, so you might as well quit. You see, it's all part of his plan to keep you from owning your own home, finding a good husband or wife, and having a family. He wants you to think that you don't deserve the good things in life. But God wants to bless all of His children.

The Bible says that a good man leaves an inheritance to his children and his children's children (Proverbs 13:22). If the enemy can make you think that you are nothing but a grasshopper, then he will keep you

> ...a good man leaves an inheritance to his children and his children's childre n
> Proverbs 13:22

from owning property, and he'll keep you from passing on an inheritance to your children. You are not a grasshopper, you are a royal priesthood. It's time to get rid of a "leftovers" mentality.

If you think you are nothing but a grasshopper, you will marry a person that is beneath you. If you don't think you have much to offer, you'll marry someone who will treat you poorly. If you don't have a good opinion of yourself, there is no sin you can't fall into. If you don't think much of yourself, you'll go out with somebody else's spouse. When you have a grasshopper mentality, you will settle for leftovers.

I can always tell what single people think of themselves by the people they date. Anytime someone has a grasshopper mentality, they'll go out with people that degrade them. If you are continually drawn to people that treat you poorly, it's simply because you don't think much of yourself, and that's why you have to know who you are in Christ. You have to change the things that you are saying about yourself. You have to read books that raise your self-esteem. You have to get into the Word of God so you will know who you are in Christ.

> ...if you are going to soar with the eagles, you have to walk away from the prairie chickens.

Now that the Greater One lives in you, you should soar with the eagles, and if you are going to soar with the eagles, you have to walk away from the prairie chickens. Sometimes you have to walk away from people who would pull you back into the failures of your past. Sometimes you have to say goodbye to people you love because you are determined not to go back to your past.

The Bible tells us not to be unequally yoked. If you are going to overcome the failures of past relationships, you have to learn to quit going out with folk who don't believe the Word of God like you do. Your flesh wants to take short cuts, but you have to make up your mind to do it God's way if you are going to be blessed.

God's order is for every man to be submitted to God first and foremost. Next, God's order is for every man to be the spiritual head of his household. And then God's order is for every wife to be yielded

> *Your flesh wants to take short cuts, but you have to make up your mind to do it God's way if you are going to be blessed.*

to her husband. And ladies, if you marry a man who is not submitted to God first, you are going to live an unhappy life. The purpose of premarital counseling is to help you see what you can't see, and face what you don't want to face. It allows you the avenue to make the needed changes before the wedding, because if the changes don't happen before you get married, there is an even lesser chance they'll change afterward.

Now that you love the Lord, things are changing. That's why you need to change your phone number. You can't take any chances of going back to your past. You need to make up your mind that you are not going back anymore. You are not going back to the sin that God brought you out of, and you're not going back to the legalism of the church you left either. You're not going back to that low self-esteem, and you are not going back to the failures of your past. You're not going back to the bars, you're not going back to the drugs or drinking, you're not going back to that old way of life. As long as I put God first in every area of my life, I know that I will live a blessed life.

> *If you are constantly being defeated, you have to stop and say, 'Wait a minute, is there something in my life that I need to change?"*

The people of God were greatly outnumbered as they approached Jericho. But they trusted God with all of their might. They praised the Lord until God brought a great victory for them. Even if the odds are completely against you, you have to know, "If God be for you, who can be against you?" (Romans 8:31). They won a mighty victory in Jericho, they shouted and the walls came down, and they had a great victory. Then they went on to a little city called Ai, an insignificant place. But they were defeated, and God said it was because there was sin in the camp. You have to look at your own life. If you are constantly being defeated, you have to stop and say, "Wait a minute, is there something in my life that I need to change?"

God sent the twelve spies into the Promised Land in

order to bring back a report to all of God's people. Two came back with a good report, and they eventually took the Promised Land. Ten came back with a negative report, and they died in the wilderness and all of their kinfolk with them. When the twelve spies came back from spying the Promised Land, they brought fruit with them.

See, God wants you to know He has some fruit waiting for you, blessings waiting for you, miracles, financial breakthroughs, healing, a spouse. In due season, you shall reap your harvest, if you don't give up.

> *God wants you to know He has some fruit waiting for you, blessings waiting for you, miracles, financial breakthroughs, healing, a spouse...*

Some people have never known anything but failure in their lives. That's because they won't believe the promises of God, and when things get tough, they give in to their flesh instead of going on and trusting God. "Oh, I did it my way." Honey, that's the problem, you did it your way. "If I will diligently obey (that doesn't mean sometimes) the Lord my God and am careful to do all that He says, He'll command the blessings on me" (Deuteronomy 28:1,8). God wants you to know that His blessings are waiting on you. All you have to do to overcome the spirit of failure is put Him first, trust in Him, don't give into your flesh, and keep on walking with the Lord.

He will work it out.

The people of God lived in the wilderness for forty years because they would not walk in faith. They lived in the wilderness because they would not believe the promises of God. God loved them, and He met their needs, but they wandered around in circles for forty years. He allowed them to live under a spirit of failure all their lives. He loved them,

> *You have to make up your mind to have a good report when you don't feel like having a good report.*

but they never had success because they wouldn't change. They were murmurers and backbiters, and they fell into sin every time they turned around.

You have to make up your mind to have a good report when you don't feel like having a good report. You have to quit your backbiting if you are going to go into the promises of God. Oh, I know you're right, and they are wrong, but you have to shut your backbiting mouth and stop your negative talk, even if you are the wife of a deacon or elder in the church.

You have to know that when you are walking with the Lord, God will eventually cause you to win. In fact, God does His best work when it looks like you can't make it. God does His best work when the odds are against you. God does His best work when it's your midnight hour. See, it was midnight when Paul and Silas began to praise the Lord. The odds were against them, and everything looked impossible, but when they had enough faith to praise, the Lord God showed up. He may not come when you want Him to come, but He always shows up on time. You need to know that God does His best work at midnight. He's always an on-time God.

> *If you'll put the Lord first in your life, He'll help you overcome all the failures of your past.*

If you'll put the Lord first in your life, He'll help you overcome all the failures of your past. If you'll put Him first, He'll help you overcome a victim mentality or a grasshopper mentality. No matter how much rejection you have gone through in your life, if you'll put the Lord first, He'll reverse the curse. If you have been beaten down in your past, it is crucial for you to understand that "Greater is He [Christ] that lives in you than he [satan] that lives in the world" (1 John 4:4). And when I'm putting God first, it's only a matter of time until He turns everything around. "In due season I will reap my harvest as long as I don't grow weary in well doing" (Galatians 6:9).

You have to know that God made you to be a giant

killer. He made you to overcome all the failures in your past. He made you to speak to every mountain and command it to come down. He made you to speak to every sickness and command it to go. You are not a nobody, not a grasshopper, you are somebody in Christ!

> *You see, the enemy doesn't fight anybody unless they have great potential. You must be going somewhere with the Lord, why else would the devil be fighting you so hard?*

If you've had a lot of rejection in your life, that tells me a whole lot about you. You see, the enemy doesn't fight anybody unless they have great potential. You must be going somewhere with the Lord, why else would the devil be fighting you so hard? The enemy wants you to think that you're not worth much. That's why you have to know who you are in Christ. You have to believe, know, and claim, "I am more than a conqueror through Christ Jesus who loves me" (Romans 8:37).

Now that you love the Lord, you have great potential. Even if you've gone through a lot in your life, God's in the process of taking what the enemy meant to destroy you and He is turning it for your good. You must get the Word of God in your heart. You see, once you are built up in the Word, and you are walking by faith, you know that the best is none too good for you.

When you get full of the Word of God, and folk tell you that you are no good, you won't believe what they say because you'll have hidden the Word of God in your heart. "God's Word is mighty and powerful and sharper than any two- edged sword" (Hebrews 4:12). "The grass withers and the flower fades but the Word of God stands forever"1 Peter 1:24-25). "Heaven and earth shall pass away, but My words shall never pass away" (Matthew 24:35). The Word of God will change you and your situation.

Now that you love the Lord, you have to understand that there is too much Blood over your life to allow the devil to keep on winning. You must believe that you are better than your past, and you must realize that you cannot settle for leftovers anymore. You are valuable, God loves you, you're a holy nation, you have great potential, and God is going to do great things in your life.

> *You must believe that you are better than your past, and you must realize that you cannot settle for leftovers anymore. You are valuable...*

Some time ago we were ministering in a church in Crawford, Mississippi. Outside of the church was this little raggedy dog with floppy ears. Just a raggedy old dog of some kind. It came up to us and just kissed us and loved on us. We went into the church, and my wife asked, "Whose dog is that?" The Bishop said he thought that it was a stray dog because it had been hanging around the church for a couple of months.

So my wife said, "Honey, I really like that dog." I said, "Ya, you like any dog." She said, "No, I like this dog." After the service, we were getting in the car, and my wife told the Bishop she wanted to take the dog home if it really was a stray. The Bishop wasn't confident it was a stray, and so he wanted to check around. A few days later he sent the dog to us. She was so sweet and happy. But, a few days after we had her, she started to sleep a lot. We'd wake her up, and she would kiss us and be so happy, then she'd go right back to sleep.

We knew something was wrong, so we took her to the vet. They determined that she was only 6 months old and that she had developed a type of tick disease, was terribly malnourished, and quite possibly may not live. In an effort to save her, the vet began to feed her intravenously and give her medication.

We had found this wonderful little stray puppy, but it didn't look as if the puppy was going to make it. So we began to pray. Now let me tell you, God is not only concerned about you, He is also concerned about anything that belongs to you. A day went by, and we still didn't know if she was going to make it, and, of course, the vet had been very negative about the whole situation.

I woke up the next day mad. Do you know what I'm talking about? I woke up mad because I felt that the devil was trying steal what belonged to us. I began to pray in a whole new way. Then my wife discovered this dog was a hunting dog called a Treeing Walker. One of the doctor's at the vet clinic remarked that the dog's marking were very rare and considered very valuable for that breed. God used that to help me with something. I realized that this wasn't just an old stray raggedy dog, this was a valuable dog. This dog had great potential. This dog was something special!

I am writing this to tell you what else I learned. You are not just an old stray, you are special, and God has a great plan for you! You're no longer a raggedy old nothing. God has a special plan for your life. You're now part of the royal priesthood and a holy nation. You are somebody! You may be crying yourself to sleep, but you are somebody. You may be depressed today, but you are somebody. It's time to dry your tears and know that in Christ Jesus you are somebody. Anyhow, our little Mississippi church dog was healed and has knit herself right into our hearts.

I am reminded of the story about Michelangelo buying an inferior piece of marble. His friends asked him why he bought that piece of marble with all of the flaws in it. He said, "Because I can see an angel locked up in the marble." You may not believe that you're an angel, but God sees something in you that you don't see.

Forget what lies behind, and reach forward for the things that lie ahead. It's time to possess all of the promises of God.

You are not ugly. God made you to be beautiful just like you are. You are unique and beautiful just like you are. Your nose and lips are just right. Your hair is just right. Your color is exactly the way God wanted you.

Let me tell you, our God is a faithful God. He never dwells on the things of the past. That's why God tells us to quit dwelling on it too. Just let go of the past and start making some new plans. Forgive everybody who has hurt you, and trust God for a new thing. Forget what lies behind, and reach forward for the things that lie ahead. It's time to possess all of the promises of God. It's your time to be blessed.

2

OVERCOMING THE SPIRIT OF FAILURE

The children of Israel came out of Egypt as dejected slaves who thought of themselves as inferior to the Egyptians. Because of the mistreatment and oppression they received, they found it hard to trust God. Their attitude was, "We can't make it." But you have to know that when you come into the family of God, everything can change. The enemy's plan is for you to be so beat down in life that you end up hating yourself. He wants you to have such low self-worth that you think you can't make it. The Bible says, "As a man thinketh in his heart, so is he" (Proverbs 23:7). In other words, the children of God thought of themselves as grasshoppers and that's exactly what they became.

You will become whatever you think about yourself. If you think of yourself as inferior, you will have an inferiority complex. If you feel like a loser, that's exactly what you'll become. The spirit of failure will dog you all of your life until you understand who you are in Christ. If you think you are no good, then there is no sin that you are not capable of falling into. If you always feel unworthy, then you will live beneath the privileges God has for you. If you think you are not valuable, then you will settle for leftovers all of your life.

> Even those closest to you might make you think that you're a nobody.

Even those closest to you might make you think that you're a nobody. If the enemy can make you think that you're no good, then you could be a low achiever all of your life. If he can make you think there's no use in trying, then he'll keep you from owning your own house. He'll even keep you from marrying a good person. The fact is, if you don't think you are a person of value, you'll marry somebody that will treat you like a dog. The spirit of failure will try and make you content with leftovers.

If you were raised by parents who encouraged you, then you are truly a blessed person. Most folk were raised by people who told them they were stupid or told them they couldn't do anything right. If you don't have a good opinion about yourself, you might not make it into your Promised Land. If you don't have a high self-worth, you'll never have the blessings that God has for you. "Beloved, I pray above all things that ye prosper and be in health even as thy soul prospers" (3 John 1:2). God desires the best for you.

Maybe you've never been told how valuable you are? Maybe nobody's ever told you that you have great potential? If that's the case, then you really need to get into the Word and know who you are in Christ. God doesn't make junk. You are now a part of the royal family. You're a part of a royal priesthood and a holy nation (1 Peter 2:9). Now that you're part of

> *Now that you're a part of the royal family, God made you to soar with the eagles (Isaiah 40:31)*

the royal family, God made you to soar with the eagles (Isaiah 40:31). He made you to be more than a conqueror (Romans 8:37). You are no longer a victim, and you are now overcoming all of your past through the Lord.

Sometimes you need to change the things you're saying about yourself. Stop cutting yourself down, quit talking negative about yourself. Even if your earthly father doesn't love you, you are of infinite value. Even if your earthly father can't show you love, you still have enormous potential because

of the greater One who lives in you. Even if your earthly
father rejects you, don't let it get you down. Just know that
the Lord loves you no matter what, and He has a great plan
for your life.

> Thinking properly about yourself is the key to this transformation process.

No matter what kind of damage
has been done in your life, whether it
was done through society or your
family, if you sell out to the Lord, He
will reverse all the damage in your life,
all the damage in your past, and help
you overcome the spirit of failure. I know you've been a
victim to your past, but when you know who you are in Christ,
something inside of you says, "I know I can make it and I'm
tired of leftovers. I'm ready to have God's best."

Begin to confess with your mouth today. Because you
are more than a conqueror, you're in the process of
overcoming all of the low self-esteem in your life. You are in
the process of overcoming all of the fears, rejection and all
the failures from your past. Thinking properly about yourself
is the key to this transformation process. Stop letting people
define who you are, and let God's Word tell you who you
are.

If you are continually drawn to people that are not good
for you, you need to get before God and say, "God, I need

You to change me." You need to talk to God about your self-esteem and find out from the Word what God says about you. Then begin to say and believe what God says about you, and not what others have said about you. When you ask Jesus to be the Lord of your life, He can turn anything around if you will ask Him.

> Get serious in prayer. Fall on your face before God and say, "God, I need You to help me. God, I need You to change me."

Death and life are in the power of your tongue (Proverbs 18:21). It's not what enters a man's mouth that defiles him; it's what comes out of his mouth that defiles him (Matthew 15:11). You will eventually have what you say. And that's why you must make up your mind to say what God says, not what society says about you.

Begin to read books about self-esteem and getting your past behind you. Start working on you. "Study to show yourself approved" (2 Timothy 2:15). Get serious in prayer. Fall on your face before God and say, "God, I need You to help me. God, I need You to change me."

Even after I was saved, I ran around with people who were not good for me. I did the same things even after I dedicated my life to the Lord, but one day something happened inside of me. I realized that I was better than my past, and I realized birds of a feather flock together. That meant that I had to change things and stop flocking together with some of the birds I'd been hanging out with.

Growing up in Christ means making tough decisions. It means making changes when you really don't want to make changes. If you are going to soar with the eagles, you must quit hanging around the sparrows and the buzzards. You must quit hanging around people that aren't going anywhere or doing anything with their lives. You must stop hanging around people that aren't putting God first, because they'll pull you down to where they are.

> You must quit hanging around people that aren't going anywhere or doing anything with their lives.

One day I read in the Word of God that I was a fellow heir and a joint heir with Jesus Christ (Romans 8:17). Whatever belongs to Jesus now belongs to me. All of a sudden it hit me who I was in Christ. I began to have a whole different set of values about who I was. I realized that everything had changed since coming to the Lord. I found out that God made me to be a giant killer. I found out that God made me to overcome my past and to defeat every obstacle that comes my way. I found out that God wants me to be blessed, and He delights in the prosperity of His servant.

Since I am serving Him, then I believe that He wants me to be blessed.

You won't have a trouble-free life just because you come to Jesus Christ. So you must make up your mind that you're going to conquer every obstacle that comes your way. Obstacles like the spirit of failure that's been on your family for generations and has now come down to you. You must make up your mind that you're going to live above the mess and live above your past.

> You won't have a trouble-free life just because you come to Jesus Christ. So you must make up your mind that you're going to conquer every obstacle that comes your way.

Let me tell you a story about rejection. Joseph came from a dysfunctional family. His father had children by four different women. His family was full of jealousy, bitterness, and hatred. His brothers threw him into a pit and tried to kill him. The family that should have loved and protected him, abused him and threw him away. But even when life was unfair to Joseph, he never became dysfunctional himself. He always trusted God and stayed faithful, and God helped him.

So if you've been rejected by those who should have loved you, just know that God is going to make it up to you as long as you put Him first and stay faithful. Joseph spent twelve years in prison for something that he did not do, but God made it up to him before it was over. He's going to do the same things in your life. God took what the devil meant to destroy Joseph and turned it for his good.

Unfortunately, some people love you only when you do well. They reject you and push you away if you don't live up to what they want you to do. Some folk love you when you smell good, but when you've got the stink of this world on you, they just push you away and reject you. The truth is that God's love is unconditional. He's going to love you just like you are.

> *Unfortunately, some people love you only when you do well. They reject you and push you away if you don't live up to what they want you to do.*

Don't worry if you feel unworthy today, we all feel that way from time to time. Just remember, it's the Blood of Jesus Christ that covers all the guilt of your past. You are now the righteousness of God through the Blood of Jesus Christ. You're in right standing before God the Father because of what Jesus Christ did on the cross. Now you've received the benefit of what He has done, and you're somebody because of that. If you are washed in the Blood, you have to understand that you are better than your past. You may have a poor self-image today, but you don't have to live like a grasshopper all your life. You can rise above your past, you can leave the prairie chickens behind, and you can soar with the eagles. You can overcome the spirit of failure, and you can have the best in your life.

> *The devil's plan is to use people to hold you down all of your life. He wants to make certain that others make you feel bad about yourself and produce in you a lifelong spirit of failure.*

Jesus said that the greatest commandment in the Bible is to love the Lord your God with all your heart, and then love your neighbor as yourself (Matthew 22:37-39). You must learn to put God first, and learn to love the people who have hurt you. Once you love the Lord with all of your heart and then love people that have hurt you, you will learn to love yourself.

The devil's plan is to use people to hold you down all of your life. He wants to make certain that others make you feel bad about yourself and produce in you a lifelong spirit of failure. No matter what people have done to you, Jesus came to set the record straight. He came to release you from all the chains of your past, and He came to set you free from every part of your past. In Luke 4:18, Jesus says this of His mission: "The Spirit of the Lord is upon me, because he hath anointed me to preach the gospel to the poor; he hath sent me to heal the brokenhearted, to preach deliverance to the captives, and recovering of sight to the blind, to set at liberty them that are bruised." He came to raise up those who are beaten down and oppressed by the devil.

> Know who you are in the Lord, raise your head up, throw your shoulders back, get a spring in your step, and celebrate who you are.

You can overcome the spirit of failure. You can get this thing turned around. You may be walking through the house crying because somebody doesn't like you. You may be depressed because folk are talking about you. It's time to dry your tears and move on with your life. Don't allow people's opinions to control you. Know who you are in the Lord, raise your head up, throw your shoulders back, get a spring in your step, and celebrate who you are.

After the city of Ziklag was burned to the ground, all the people wanted to kill David. So David had to encourage himself because he had no one around him who could. Like David, there's going to come a time in your life when you will have no one to encourage you, but you. And that's when you'll have to open up your mouth and say aloud what God says about you. "I am the righteousness of God. Folk may be against me, they may be lying about me, but I know who I am in Christ. I'm going somewhere with my life. I will not live with leftovers all of my life."

Make no mistake, we all know it hurts when those close to you don't believe in you. I wish I could say that eventually you get to the point that nothing ever bothers you. Make up your mind in advance that you are not going to let it slow you down. That's when you just have to say, "God, I give it to you, I'm going to trust in you, I'm going to release this thing into your hands."

Quit wasting your life living in the failures of your past. It's time to serve an eviction notice on the devil. It's time to overcome the low self-esteem of your past, get over it, get on with your life, and trust God to rebuild. Maybe you need

> *Quit wasting your life living in the failures of your past. It's time to serve an eviction notice on the devil.*

to know why someone doesn't love you anymore? Or perhaps you need to understand why your parents put you up for adoption? But, there are some things you're never going to figure out. And all you can do is say, "God, I put it in Your hands; I'm turning it loose, and I'm walking away. I'm going on with my life.

There is greatness inside of you. Because of your past, you may not believe me, you may think that's just preacher talk, but that's Bible talk, and Bible truth. Maybe you did mess up a lot and because you messed up, all your family did was talk negative about you? You can get it turned around. If you will obey God, and understand who you are in Christ, you can give up the leftovers of your past, and have God's best.

3

OVERCOMING FAILURE IN RELATIONSHIPS

Whether you know it or not, we all need to make changes in our lives, especially in our relationships. And, more specifically, we need to make changes in our relationship with the Lord. Since God has called all men to be the spiritual head of their household, men must take the lead spiritually in their homes. This isn't an act of seizing power; it's a lifelong attitude of sacrificial leadership for the benefit of the whole family. Yet for many men it's easier to relinquish spiritual leadership to their wives because they are busy trying to build a career, make money, and advance in their profession.

God has called every man to wash his wife and his family in the water of the Word every day. Every man is supposed to get up and pray over his family. God has called every husband to be the spiritual leader in his home, the *house band*. He is to be the one that leads his family in the way they should go. God has called every wife to be the support for the husband as the spiritual head. Men you need to learn to take the spiritual lead, and ladies you need to learn to be a prayer support and let your man lead. The Holy Spirit is the helper of the Godhead, the wife is to be the helper to her husband. The woman is the one called alongside to help him.

> *God is looking for a man to build up a hedge of righteousness over his family through prayer.*

God is looking for a man to build up a hedge of righteousness over his family through prayer. God is looking for men to pray over their families so destruction can be diverted. Men, if you want to overcome the spirit of failure in your household, become the spiritual head of your family and take the lead in prayer. If you're going to overcome the spirit of failure from your past, you must make up your mind to take the lead. A good man takes the lead in his family. A good man prays over his family. A good man leaves an inheritance to his children and his children's children. A good man pays his bills. A good man trusts God. A good man is in church.

The man is to submit to God, and the wife is to yield to her husband. He is to be the quarterback, and she is to throw blocks for him from time to time. She is to be the support. When a woman enters into marriage, she has to enter in with a whole lot more faith than her husband does. She must learn to back up and keep her mouth shut even when she may know more than he does.

When a wife yields to the authority of her husband, she is honoring God. If you don't understand anything else, wives, please understand this. When a wife yields to her husband, she is saying, "God, I will obey You. It is very difficult at times, but I will obey You." It takes great faith for a wife to yield to her husband, especially when she thinks he is wrong.

> *When a wife yields to the authority of her husband, she is honoring God.*

Some wives will not yield to their husbands until they feel their husbands' lives are right with God. Yet, when a wife yields to her husband, his heart is more easily turned towards God.

God has called the husband to lead the team, but he can't lead if the wife won't follow. Even if he makes mistakes, God has called him to lead. The reason why some women are angry today is because men won't take the lead. God never called women to lead their families. God never called women to be the breadwinners of the family. God never called women to fight devils over their children. God called the men to do all of that. But there cannot be peace in the home if two people are trying to lead. Somebody has to lead, and somebody has to say, "Okay, I'm going to follow." There has to be headship, and then there has to be support for the headship.

> The reason some folk keep living under a spirit of failure is because their house is out of order.

The reason some folk keep living under a spirit of failure is because their house is out of order. God has called men to be the primary disciplinarians, not the women. He's called the men to take the lead in raising their families. He called the men to lay hands on the children. He's called men to pray.

God has called the man to be the protector. He's called the man to be the provider. He is to love his wife as Christ loved the church. He is to provide vision for the family. When a man is fulfilling his destiny he'll be full of goals, dreams and vision. When he has the strength and support of a loving wife, he is unstoppable. As a team, when a man and woman are submitted to God properly, they can accomplish anything.

Where any two agree as touching anything, it shall be done for them. That's why the devil is always trying to cause division in your home. A house divided cannot stand.

The woman was created by God to be a helper for her husband. She was pulled out of man not to be his slave, but to assist him in every way. One of the ways she assists her husband is in promoting godly principles in the home. But before you think God's ideal female is just this real nice, sweet Christian woman whose motto is "please walk all over me", you need to hear what God says about the godly woman in Proverbs 31.

> *A Godly woman is a woman with goals and abilities. She gets up and takes care of her family. She's got her own businesses that give her independent streams of income.*

A Godly woman is a woman with goals and abilities. She gets up and takes care of her family. She's got her own businesses that give her independent streams of income. She's got everything going on in her own life, but although she has numerous interests, she is family-centered. Her children and her husband shower her with praise. She trusts God. She puts God first. She is all of that and more! So, whenever you need a reminder of what the godly woman looks like, read Proverbs 31 again.

God made man out of the dust of the earth, but woman was pulled out of man and that's why she constantly looks to man for protection and security. Men, you must understand the differences between men and women. Women need security. A man can go from job to job. He can live in one apartment and then another one. He can move from city to city and not even think about it. But a woman needs her nest. She needs her home. She needs that place of security that she knows she can trust in. That's why it's so important for a man to understand he must build security for his wife. A woman needs to know that her husband is going to take care of her. She needs to know that he'll go to battle for her. She needs to know that he can pay the bills.

> *I know they think they're going to change them after they get married, but it probably won't happen...*

The reason God tells you not to be going out with unsaved people is because if you marry you're going to have a difficult life. Why? Because you're not going to be thinking the same, your goals are not going to be the same, and you are not going to have the spirit of unity. I'm telling you that dating unbelievers is crazy because what you see is what you get. I know they think they're going to change them after they get married, but it probably won't happen.

God has called men to be the visionaries of the family. Men, that's why you must tell your wife how you're going to get out of debt. You're supposed to be the visionary, the man with a plan. You must tell her how you're going to get that house. You must tell her how you're going to raise the kids. Without a vision, the people will perish (Proverbs 29:18). You must spread the vision to your wife and then to the kids.

> *Ladies, if you have your eye on a man who doesn't work, he is not your man. You want somebody with vision;*

God put the man in the garden, and He told him to work the garden. Ladies, if you have your eye on a man who doesn't work, he is not your man. You want somebody with vision; you want somebody who's a hard worker. You don't want somebody who's just talking about it; you want somebody who will get out and do it. That's why in the dating process you have to take your time. We men can hide who we really are for quite some time.

God put the man in the garden and told him to cultivate it. He was to bring the best out of his garden. That's what God wants from each man today. He wants you to bring the best out of your family. Be an encourager of your family. Lead by example. Don't just send your children to church, take them to church. They need to see you tithe, they need to see you praise and worship God.

If the husband nourishes his wife spiritually, she will flourish under his leadership. If a husband is nourishing his wife properly, she will look better after they are married than before. If your wife doesn't look better now, you must take the responsibility yourself. Quit blaming her. You must be careful of the way you talk to her, the tone of voice that you use with her. You must be careful of the way you treat her.

> When my wife took my name, she became an extension of me. Now everywhere she goes, she represents me.

When my wife took my name, she became an extension of me. Now everywhere she goes, she represents me. I want her to look as good as she can look. She is representing me and that's why I do everything I can to treat her good. That's why you must set aside your stingy self and take care of your wife before you take care of yourself.

Do you know the story about the eagles that are dating? A male eagle is courting a female who isn't paying any attention to him because she thinks he's just full of talk. Eventually she picks up a stick and drops it. Now if he lets the stick hit the ground, he's toast. She's done with him, and she's not even going on a first date. So, he flies down and catches it. And then she begins testing the boy with more sticks. Each stick is bigger and heavier and harder to handle. He has to catch each stick before it hits the ground because she's trying to find out if he can take care of their family in the future. That's why the dating process is so important when you are single. You need to find out if that person is capable of meeting your needs in the future.

> *If you're single and looking for a spouse, you shouldn't marry somebody who's not already happy. If you become someone else's source of happiness, they'll drain the life out of you.*

You must learn about meeting each other's needs. That's why it's so important not to have sex in the dating process. Once you start having sex, your brain turns to mush. Ladies, you need a warrior not mama's boy. Quit picking up the dinner tab just so he'll go out with you. Girl just slow down and wait and see what he's going to do. You can do bad all by yourself.

If you're single and looking for a spouse, you shouldn't marry somebody who's not already happy. If you become someone else's source of happiness, they'll drain the life out of you. You cannot become anybody's God, only the Lord can be their God. You must learn to be happy while you're single, or you'll never be happy after you're married. Quit waiting to get married to be happy. Enjoy your life now. Go places now. Go do things now. Go to the movies, go camping, go someplace. If you need a little more love, buy yourself a dog.

If you're dating someone right now who doesn't build you up, you'd better walk away.

If you're dating someone right now who doesn't build you up, you'd better walk away. Almost all of us have low self-esteem to some degree. And we need all the encouragement we can get. We don't need to get hooked up with somebody who can't encourage us. Ladies, if he can't nourish and cherish you while you're single, he'll never do it after you are married. You can't take the first person that comes along. And just because you meet him in church doesn't mean God sent him to you. He could be sitting right next to you in church just playing the game. You don't need any more Mac Daddies in your life.

If they're talking down to you now while you are single, you'd better run away as fast as you can. In Christ you are somebody. In Christ you are better than that. If you are willing and obedient, then you will have the best of the land.

If you don't know who you are in Christ, you may be

attracted to the wrong kind of people. When you have a low self-image and somebody really nice comes along, you're not interested. You don't even notice them. Instead, you keep looking around for freaky Freddie or Raunchy Rita who never calls and treats you like dirt. You need to know you're better than all of that. You like Slick Sammy and Sexy Susie, and you know they're the one who stole that money from you. You can do bad all by yourself. You are better than that, you deserve God's best.

You may be content to just live with somebody, but you have to know you're better than that. God gave you the marriage covenant as a means of protection. You see, God cannot bless shacking up because it's outside of His plan. He said if you will diligently obey the Lord your God and be careful to do all that He says, He'll command the blessing on you.

> *The marriage covenant is about one man and one woman becoming one flesh. In other words, when we are one flesh we don't have separate bank accounts.*

The marriage covenant is about one man and one woman becoming one flesh. In other words, when we are one flesh we don't have separate bank accounts. Now I know why people have separate bank accounts, but I'm telling you, one flesh does not have separate bank accounts. One flesh does not go on separate vacations. One flesh does not have boys' night or girls' night out. I know it's tight, but it's still right.

When you get married, you give up your independence. Now I didn't say that you give up your individuality. You keep your individuality, but you give up your independence. If you cannot give up your independence, what are you doing getting married? Your marriage will always live under a spirit of failure as long as you live under that spirit of independence.

> The Bible says that when the two of you entered into a marriage covenant you became one flesh (Genesis. 2:24). It's God's desire that you give up your individual selfish desires.

The Bible says that when the two of you entered into a marriage covenant you became one flesh (Genesis. 2:24). It's God's desire that you give up your individual selfish desires. He wants you to come together with one common goal or purpose while honoring God and putting Him first. Then you can work toward your dream together.

Men and women are so different. They hear love differently. Men need to be admired and respected while women need an abundance of love. Men need a great amount of physical pleasure while women need a great amount of security and emotional support. So, if you and your partner give each other what you need, everything can change for the better. If you're going to see healing in any relationship, you must be determined to meet the other person's needs.

When marriages are in trouble, it's because somebody's needs are not being met. When your partner gets what they need, they are more capable of meeting your needs. Remember the Word of God, "Give, and it shall be given unto you, good measure, pressed down, and shaken together, running over" (Luke 6:38).

It's God's desire that we bring healing to one another. We need to be understanding. We need to be gentle. There should never be a question about loyalty in your relationship whether you are single or married. If there is a question about loyalty, you have big troubles. But when you meet the other person's needs, they will do more to meet your needs.

If your spouse feels as though you're unhappy with him or her, it's going to build insecurity. If your spouse does not feel your support, it's only a matter of time until you're under a spirit of failure. Hurting people always hurt people. Hurting people don't even know they hurt people. They're hurting so much themselves that they don't know what they are doing.

There is something inside all of us that longs to be loved by one special person, and because of that need to be loved, we tend to do stupid things. We tend to try to rush the case. We tend to be needy ourselves. We need to make up our minds that we are not going to have sex outside of marriage. You see, once sex enters a relationship, everything begins to change. It's important in the dating process that you become best friends. If you start having sex, that friendship thing stops.

> *Peter tells husbands they need to love their wives in an understanding way. If your wife had a harsh father, then you need to learn to lower your voice. Learn to be gentler.*

May I also say to the ladies, you need to be careful about the way you dress? You cannot trust men. We love God, but we are very sexual, and we are very visually oriented. If you have the neckline plunged way down and your dress hiked way up, I am telling you that you will entice him with your body, and that's all you will ever have.

Peter tells husbands they need to love their wives in an understanding way. If your wife had a harsh father, then you need to learn to lower your voice. Learn to be gentler. God said, unless you give your wife honor He won't answer your prayers. If your wife had an abusive previous marriage, you need to focus on building security in her life.

Ten years ago I was insecure in some areas that are not an issue for me now. By the same token, I have insecure areas in my life today that I didn't have ten years ago. My wife knows that and she helps me with it. But you must learn the strengths and weaknesses of your spouse or the person you're dating. Begin to communicate by talking about those problem areas so you can strengthen one another.

Men, even though you're the leader, you must quit making all the decisions by yourselves. If you will bring your wife into the decision-making process, she will feel valued. You will gain from her input and the benefit of her woman's intuition. Believe me, getting her opinion will keep you out of a lot of trouble.

> *Talk about your needs when it's appropriate. When you're in a marriage relationship that isn't meeting your needs, you can feel trapped and depressed.*

Talk about your needs when it's appropriate. When you're in a marriage relationship that isn't meeting your needs, you can feel trapped and depressed. Talk about it without accusing your partner. Let me tell you, if you discover your spouse is depressed but you can't figure out why, I just gave you the answer: unmet needs.

The Bible says, "Death and life are in the power of the tongue" (Proverbs 18:21). You can bring healing to your relationship if you'll quit being negative to each other, if you'll stop criticizing each other, and if you'll speak life and love to one another. Keep in mind that people tend to live up to (or down to) what you say and believe about them.

Overcome the spirit of failure by learning to call things that be not as though they were. Start saying, "Baby, you are so fine." Start saying, "You're the greatest thing in my life!", even when you don't feel it. Be positive and expect God to work when you obey Him and seek to do His will.

You can bring healing to your situation if you'll stop trying to change your mate. Start meeting your mate's needs, and as you do, your mate will start meeting your needs. As that begins to work its way into your mindset and relationship, you'll begin to see changes taking place. But you must be patient, because changes in relationships do not take place overnight.

The right kind of man will encourage his wife and bring healing to her. The right kind of woman will encourage her man and bring healing to him. "One can put a thousand to flight, but two can put ten thousand to flight" (Deuteronomy 32:30). There are some things you cannot get done by yourself. I don't care how strong you are, you need each other far more than you think you do.

If you're in a relationship today, and things aren't working, you must be willing to say that you will do whatever you have to do to make this thing work out. If you are married, and things aren't working, you need to look at the way you treat each other. Look at the way you talk to each other. We all have certain needs in relationships. Love me the way I need to be loved, not the way you think I need to be loved. Touch me the way I need to be touched. Talk to me the way I need to be talked to. Build security in me the way I need it.

God can't heal your relationship until you are willing to make some changes. I'm talking about things like sending her flowers for no reason, calling her on the phone in the middle of the day, or telling her you are sorry for being so harsh. Many men don't have the courage to apologize or say they are sorry, you'll be a cut above the crowd if you do.

> *Don't let your words destroy your family. Stop telling your children they will never amount to anything.*

Don't let your words destroy your family. Stop telling your children they will never amount to anything. Stop telling your husband he's no good. In the marriage covenant, your spouse should know that you have their back covered, that you will never undermine, belittle, or demean them.

Your spouse should know that you are there to stay. Never threaten, "I want a divorce." That is just an attempt to control your partner through fear and insecurity. When you say, "I want a divorce" all you do is bring more instability into an already shaky situation. Your spouse and your family need to know that you are going to be there come hell or high water.

We're supposed to bring reassurance to our spouses or to those we are dating. If you make your husband feel as though he does not make enough money, you're going to create insecurity in him. It's time to wipe the slate clean. It's time to quit talking about the things you did in the past. It's time to forgive and go on. It's time to let some things go and trust God. Your attitude should be, "I can't change where I've been, but I can change where I'm going. And maybe I didn't care for your needs the way I should have, but it's a new day. I'm changing some things, and from this day forward, I'm going to encourage you in a whole new way."

> Sometimes we need to humble ourselves and say, "I'm sorry." Sometimes we need to put our arms around each other and say, "I've failed you, forgive me."

Sometimes we need to humble ourselves and say, "I'm sorry." Sometimes we need to put our arms around each other and say, "I've failed you, forgive me." It's time to forget what lies behind and reach forward to what lies ahead. It's time to drop the charges. It's time to say, "God, I'm going to do it Your way from now on. I'm tired of doing it my way. I've been doing it my way and look at the mess I made out of things. Lord, help me to do it Your way from now on. I'm tired of leftovers and I'm going to put you first."

No More Leftovers

4

DEALING WITH YOUR ANGRY SELF

Before we gave our lives to the Lord, we'd go off on people when we were angry. But now that we love the Lord, He expects us to put on the nature of Christ and walk in love. That means we have to forgive folk we don't necessarily want to forgive. That means turning the other cheek when we'd rather just cuss them out.

Now we all should understand that growing up in Christ is a process. I'm not as good as I need to be, but I'm a whole lot better than I used to be. And now He's got me on the potter's wheel, spinning me and getting that stuff out of my life.

Paul tells us about all the deeds of the flesh, and in that

he includes anger. He says that if you practice anger you will not inherit the kingdom of God. The reason you keep wandering around in the wilderness is because you aren't overcoming the works of the flesh. Rather, you give into the works of the flesh and you allow anger to control your life.

So because of your anger you stay in the wilderness, and you never quite go into the promises of God. If you allow anger to control you, you will never have God's best in your life. In fact, all you will ever have is leftovers.

> *So because of your anger, you stay in the wilderness, and you never quite go into the promises of God.*

The Bible plainly tells us, when we hold on to anger we will live in the wilderness, spiritually speaking. We will be weaker personally and less effective for the Lord. God loved Moses, but because of his anger, Moses lived in the wilderness almost all of his life. We see the first evidence of Moses' anger when, as a young man, he killed an Egyptian who was beating a Hebrew. When he realized that the incident was known, he had to flee for his life and for the next forty years he lived in the wilderness.

After this period, God called Moses to lead the Hebrew people out of slavery in Egypt and into the Promised Land of Israel. But because of the sin of unbelief by some, the whole Hebrew nation was forced to wander in the wilderness for forty years. Then, eighty years after his anger problem back in Egypt, Moses could have entered the Promised Land. But, because he hadn't learned his lesson or dealt with his anger during those eighty years, he got extremely angry when the people complained about a lack of water.

Since God had always provided for His people, Moses could not believe the people's lack of faith. But he talked to God, and God told him to speak to the rock and water would come forth, but Moses lost control, and in his anger he beat the rock with the rod instead of speaking to it. Because of this sin, he was not allowed to enter the Promised

> Anytime we give into anger, we give the devil an opportunity to destroy us.

Land. He only got to see it from a distance, and he died in the wilderness. Anytime you lose control of your temper, you are in danger of being in sin and in danger of having to live in the wilderness all of your life. Anytime you lose your temper, you are in danger of missing God's best.

Anytime we give into anger, we give the devil an opportunity to destroy us. Anytime we allow anger to control us, we open the door for the enemy to come in. Anytime we allow our anger to be out of control, it's just like we walked to the door, turned the doorknob, pulled the door wide open and said, "Come on in here devil, and steal everything I have, steal my family, steal my money! Go ahead and steal it all!"

> *If you will deal with your anger issues today, you can trust that God will help you.*

That's why we cannot let one day go by without dealing with anger issues, without letting go of the things that have hurt us and are causing us to be angry. Got an anger issue? Don't let the sun go down on your anger. Don't carry it another day.

If you will deal with your anger issues today, you can trust that God will help you. But if you don't do something now, you could live under a spirit of failure where nothing ever works out for you. It's okay to be angry with a family member, just don't let it get inside of you. It's okay to be angry with a co-worker, just don't hold things against him or her. "Be angry and sin not" (Ephesians 4:26). If you're tired of leftovers, make up your mind to let go of all of your anger issues.

One of the fruits of the spirit is self-control. If you are angry, and you let your anger get out of control, you have missed the entire message of being controlled by the spirit of God. You must control the things you say and do. It is not okay to cuss at somebody because you are mad. If you raise your voice because you are trying to make your point, you are out of control. If you explode and yell and scream, you are out of control. If you slam doors, you are out of control. But if you will confess your sin of anger, He will forgive you and help you.

> *God may be talking to you right now about coming to Him and saying, "God, I'm giving You all these anger issues in my life."*

God may be talking to you right now about coming to Him and saying, "God, I'm giving You all these anger issues in my life." The Bible says to confess your faults to one another so you may be healed. Sometimes you need to say, "You know I am really angry, but God, I'm going to give this to You because I can't take care of this myself, and I need Your strength. I can do all things through Christ who strengthens me."

The real reason you are so hot-tempered is because you've been wounded in the past, and you've never learned how to let it go. The real reason you want to fight somebody when you don't get your way is because there is something going on inside of you. You don't like yourself; and you are trying to control other people around you. You've been hurt and now you have to learn to deal with some issues that have left you with lingering pain.

You see, anger is really not about anger, it is about

control. The real reason you are so angry is because you are hurting, and you haven't resolved conflicts in your life. You need healing from those conflicts if you are going to overcome the anger issue. Sometimes you just need to take off the mask. Sometimes you must say, "God, this is really who I am, and I need Your help."

But if you can't humble yourself and take off the mask, not much will ever change in your life.

> If you're going to overcome that hot temper, you're going to have to admit your anger.

If you're going to overcome that hot temper, you're going to have to admit your anger. You're going to have to be willing to say, "Lord, I give this to You. Lord, I need You." I know you have a good excuse about why you blow your top. Yes, you have a good reason why you go off on folk, but you'll never change until you face yourself and ask for God to help you.

If you give into anger, you'll say and do things that you will regret for a long time. If you give into anger, the devil won't have to destroy you, you'll destroy yourself. In fact, if you give into anger, you'll live under a spirit of failure all of your life. You'll go from job to job because of your anger. You'll go from broken relationship to broken relationship.

Anytime someone's needs are not being met in a

relationship, anger is usually the result. Anytime someone's needs are not being met in marriage, even the smallest little thing can trigger anger. Anger comes into our lives for various reasons, and that's why you need to determine the root cause of your anger. Anger usually means there is something in your past that you haven't dealt with.

Perhaps you were abandoned or abused as a child or maybe you were sick or hurt as a child. Or, it could be that somewhere in your past you were abandoned, hurt, or abused through a relationship. You may have experienced a great injustice at some point in your life. You must have enough faith to say, "God, I give this to You." You must have enough faith to say, "God, life looks totally unfair, but I am not going to lose control, and I am going to give this to You and have enough faith to believe that You are going to work it out."

> *You must have enough faith to say, "God, I give this to You."*

Anytime somebody lets us down, it can leave us angry. If a wife is not responsive to her husband's sexual needs, he can feel real anger. When a husband does not take responsibility for raising the children and making a good living, a wife can be very insecure and angry.

What are the issues in your life? Anytime people feel cheated, they can become angry. If you lend people money and they don't repay you, it will make you angry. That's why the Word says that when you lend money to others don't expect them to pay you back. So, if you expect them to pay you back, and they ask you for money, just tell them, "No." You'll save yourself a whole lot of trouble down the road.

> *Anger results from the fact or perception that someone infringed on your rights.*

Anger results from the fact or perception that someone infringed on your rights. Somebody didn't give you what you deserve. Somebody didn't give you what you needed. Somebody cheated you out of your blessing. Do you know what I'm talking about?

Sometimes we explode because things just mount up inside of us. It's like the straw that breaks the camel's back. We put up with stuff, we put up with stuff, we put up with stuff, and somewhere along the line it reaches a point where we say, "I can't take it anymore!" and we just blow up.

Impatience will cause you to be angry. "Hurry up! I've waited long enough. Can't you do anything right?" That's why you have to be able to talk about the things that are bothering you. You must be able to communicate the issues that are getting under your skin. Rather than allowing things to build up inside like a pressure cooker, you must be able to say, "Baby, we have to talk about this. I have an issue here and this thing is getting under my skin and before it becomes a big problem, let's go ahead and talk about it right now."

> *Men are taught to not show any emotion; ...if anybody gets in your way, knock their block off.*

But of course, when it comes to communication, we men are the worst. We've probably already said our twelve thousand words before we got home so we've made our quota. We've talked all day and don't want to talk anymore. And, of course, we men don't talk many times about specific issues because of our pride. Yet we insist to everyone that we don't have pride problems. But what we really need is to learn to humble ourselves.

Men are taught to not show any emotion and if anybody gets in your way, knock their block off. We tell little Sammy, "Stand up to them. If they hurt your feelings, go take care of them." As a result, many men grow up filled with anger and are about ready to explode. But you see, anger is just like every other sin, it doesn't get better.

You can apologize to your spouse and promise a thousand times you'll never do it again, but unless you get to the root cause and deal with those specific issues, nothing will ever change. You must face it and talk about it. If you are tired of leftovers, you have to deal with specific issues and get them out in the open.

Let me tell you how men really are. He can have something bothering him and you say, "Honey, what's wrong?" What does he say? "Nothing." "Baby, is there something bothering you?" "No." And if you press him too hard he just gets up and walks out of the room. But now we have a time bomb ticking.

> *When men get hurt physically, they usually don't cry, but when they get their feelings hurt, they bottle up on the inside until they blow a fuse.*

When men get hurt physically, they usually don't cry, but when they get their feelings hurt, they bottle up on the inside until they blow a fuse. And because of men's pride they find it difficult to say, "Honey, you hurt me." When was the last time you heard a man say, "Honey, you hurt me." But that's because their pride won't let them say that. So they keep it inside until they explode.

Anytime there is domestic violence in the home, it's because somebody is trying to gain control. Whenever somebody's physically abusive, it's because in some way, fear has come in and they are afraid. Since anger is often about control, your anger comes out because you are trying to control a given situation or person.

When people get angry, their voices get louder and louder. And it's all about establishing control. When a good Christian begins to cuss like a sailor, it's not because they don't love Jesus, it's because they are trying to establish control. It's because they are afraid of not getting what they think they need. They are afraid of being alone. They are afraid that you will leave them. They are afraid of you withdrawing your love. Now that we are born again, we are supposed to trust in the Lord with all of our hearts and lean not unto our own understanding. We are supposed to put control in His hands and say, "God, I'm believing You to take care of it."

> *Now that we are born again, we are supposed to trust in the Lord with all of our hearts and lean not unto our own understanding.*

Anytime an injustice takes place, the appropriate response is anger. We ought to be angry when racism shows up. We ought to be angry when somebody is discriminated against, but we must never forget that "Vengeance is mine; I will repay, saith the Lord" (Romans 12:19). As believers we must put every situation into God's hands and forgive people. We can never let ourselves be angry and out of control.

"God, I give this to You. It's unfair but I give it to You. I don't know why You let this happen, but I'm going to give it to You."

Our prisons are full of people who allowed anger overtake them. One fit of anger can cause a person to live in the wilderness of prison all the rest of their life. Do you know that sixty percent of all homicides in America happen among family members? You must deal with your angry self. God wants you to be blessed. That's why you have to deal with anger issues so that you can have God's best.

> *You should never discipline your children when you are angry.*

Now, I need to talk to parents for just a moment. You should never discipline your children when you are angry. Yes, they need to be disciplined, but not out of anger. They need to be disciplined out of love, and since it's so hard to control your anger when you are mad, just tell them, "Wait one hour and then I'm going to deal with you." Never withdraw your love from your children when you are disciplining them.

Paul told us to give no place to the devil. Anytime we give in to anger we open the door for destruction. "Be angry and sin not." How many people will you run off before you make up your mind to change? How many broken relationships will you go through before you quit blaming everybody else?

What does it say about you if a certain person's name comes up, and you can't find anything nice to say? Sometimes you must let things go and trust God. You must forgive folk you don't want to forgive, simply because you are sick and tired of living under a spirit of failure. The truth is, anger is about self. Me. My rights are being infringed upon. God said you'd never be happy about what you get; it's what you give that's going to make you happy. But when you're walking by faith, you believe that in due season your harvest is going to come. And it doesn't matter if some folk get blessed more than you. The key is to know that as long as you diligently obey the Lord your God, your blessing is coming back to you.

If you continually suffer from depression, you can bet that you have some issues in your life that are unresolved. There's some kind of conflict in your life that is causing you to be depressed. As you begin to examine the issues in your life, you may find that the issues are not as bad as the depression indicates.

The Word of God says to take courage. Be strong in the Lord and the power of His might and trust Him in a whole new way. Many times depression is nothing more than suppressed anger. That's why you must let things go that have hurt you. Don't get upset because the evildoer is prospering more than you, they're going to be burned up one of these days. Your blessing is coming. Besides, you must believe that God is watching over everything in your life, and in due season, He will even the score. Even if life was very unfair, sometime down the road, God will even things up. He's promised to bring you your breakthrough in due season. He promised to work everything out in your life. That's the faith issue you have to contend with today.

> Whatever you do, it's necessary to resolve all of the issues and all of the conflict that has created the anger. Even if you have to visit a gravesite and say, "I forgive you for all the things in my life."

Whatever you do, it's necessary to resolve all of the issues and all of the conflict that has created the anger. Even if you have to visit a gravesite and say, "Daddy, I forgive you for all the things in my life." Even if that's what you have to do, you have to resolve the conflict. "Well, Bishop, bad tempers run in my family." They probably do because great grand-daddy had a bad temper, and he didn't deal with it. He passed it on to your daddy, who passed it on to you, and now you are passing it on to your own kids. It's time to break that generational curse.

It's time to deal with your angry family. It's time to deal with your angry self. It's time to deal with your angry past. You must forgive an ex-spouse so you can go on to build new relationships. You need to forgive your daddy so that you can quit making your spouse pay for all the things your daddy did. It's time to forgive people who have done things to you. You can't risk going on without the promises of God. You can't take any chances with your blessings. You must get out from underneath that spirit of failure that has held you down all your life. It's time for you to be willing and obedient so that you can have the best in your life.

> *It's time to deal with your angry family. It's time to deal with your angry self. It's time to deal with your angry past.*

Quit thinking of yourself as a victim. You are now more than a conqueror through Christ Jesus who loves you. You are going to rise up out of the ashes of your past. You are going to rise above all of the generational curses in your family. You are about to be blessed by God in a whole new way.

Think about this. Moses was called "a friend of God,"

and talked to God personally. Moses was God's chosen servant to bring His people out of Egypt and lead them through the wilderness for forty years. Yet the Bible says that Moses was the most humble man on earth. Even so, God would not let Moses enter the Promised Land because of one act of anger. This being true, what makes you think that you are going into your spiritual Promised Land unless you exercise your faith and deal with your angry self? What makes you thing that you are going to have the best unless you deal with your angry self?

We all have issues in our lives. But God just wants us to humble ourselves so we can say, "Honey, I've got a bad temper, and I need you to forgive me. I know I need help." That's all God is waiting on. Repent before God. Repent before your wife. Repent before your children. And watch what God does in your life and in your family's life.

5

COURAGE UNDER FIRE

God told Joshua to be strong and courageous. Now courage is about being strong even when you don't feel strong. Courage is about pressing ahead to do something even though the odds may be completely against you. Courage is not the absence of fear, it's about pressing through the fears in order to obtain the promises through faith. Fear will try to hold you back, but courage is a determination to press through the fear. As long as you don't allow fear to control your life, God will command His blessings on you. As long as you put God first, you will have God's blessing.

Eddie Rickenbacker was an American Ace, the leading American combat pilot in World War I. He downed twenty-six enemy planes. Though considered a hero by millions, Rickenbacker confessed that he was scared every time he faced the enemy in combat. You see, courage can press through all of the fears that would hold us back or intimidate us. Courage doesn't run from fear; courage knows that fear is there, but says, "I'm going to face my fear and I'm going to trust God with all of my heart."

> Courage is making up your mind to face the music rather than running away.

Courage is making up your mind to face the music rather than running away. For example, God may be calling you to preach for Him. He may be calling you to speak for Him, but fear of public speaking may hold you back. You must make up your mind to walk in courage and believe that God is with you. Courage is about confronting something or someone that you're afraid of. It's about making a career move that has frightened you in the past. It's about pressing through the fears in order to walk by faith and not by sight. As long as you let fear control your life, you'll never have God's best. If you are tired of leftovers, make a decision today to deal with the fears that are controlling you.

God doesn't want us to be fearful of anything. He wants us to cover everything with prayer and keep on walking with courage. Even when you get a bad report from your doctor, God wants you to slip on the robe of courage. He wants you to make up your mind that you are going to say the right things. You see, courage comes out in the words that you say. You must make up your mind you're going to be a person that is courageous in words and actions.

The devil's plan is for you to be afraid of people. He wants you to be afraid of situations. He wants to hold you down and keep you defeated all of your life, but God tells you to be strong and very courageous because He has promised success in your life.

> *Even when you get a bad report from your doctor, God wants you to slip on the robe of courage. He wants you to make up your mind that you are going to say the right things.*

See, you must fight for it. Simply because God says healing is yours, you can't be praying "Oh, God, if you want me to be healed, go ahead and heal me." You need to know your covenant rights. You must fight for what is yours. You must stand on the Word of God. God said that property belongs to you. That house belongs to you. But you must be courageous and fight for it. See, having courage doesn't mean you don't have fear. Having courage simply means you'll fight through the fears, you'll press ahead with faith in God in spite of the fear.

Make no mistake, your spiritual enemy has a plan for you to be fearful. As long as you walk in fear, you will never have the blessings of God. The enemy's plan is for you to never be courageous so he can cause you to live a defeated life. The enemy's plan is for you to live with leftovers all of your life. That's why you have to be determined to trust in the Lord.

> *The enemy's plan is for you to never be courageous so he can cause you to live a defeated life.*

Peter got out of the boat and began walking on the water. When he began to look at the storm around him, he became afraid. Fear came into his life, and he began to sink. That's what your spiritual enemy would like to do to you. He wants you to get your eyes off the Lord and begin to look at the trouble around you so you will begin to fail. You must make up your mind that even though a storm may come into your life, you're not going to be afraid. When you are truly trusting, you can rely on God right *in the middle of the storm.*

Make no mistake, any time you step out in faith, fear will raise its ugly head. You need to know that fear is one of Satan's greatest weapons against the children of God and that's why we must resist it. That's why we must be determined to walk in courage. Your spiritual enemy would love for you to walk in fear, because as long as you walk in fear, you'll make wrong decisions. As long as you walk in fear, you will be timid, you'll hold back, and you won't go all the way with God. That's why you have to get your eyes off of the storm and begin to get your eyes back on the Lord and trust in Him. I'm talking about having courage...courage under fire.

> *As long as you walk in fear, you will be timid, you'll hold back, and you won't go all the way with God.*

2 Timothy 1:7 says, "For my God has not given me a spirit of fear, but of power, and of love and of a sound mind." Even though fear may come against your mind, you have to be determined to continue walking in courage. Actually this Scripture is translated, "My God has not given me a spirit of timidity." I've met a lot of people that are timid. They're afraid of making a mistake. They are afraid that they are going to fail. Timidity is nothing more than fear. It's just a milder version of it.

Do you need to confront a family member? Perhaps you're afraid to confront the person because of the way he or she always explodes when you try to talk on a serious level. But whatever you do, you cannot let fear hold you hostage any longer. Whoever you need to confront today just know that you can face them with courage whether you have to face a co-worker or whether you have to confront a family member. God wants you to settle the issue and stop walking in fear. None of us like confrontation. We all want everything to go nice and smooth. You have to put on courage and make up your mind to keep walking by faith.

> *Because peer pressure can be relentless, we frequently feel a pull toward doing things that we know are wrong. It takes enormous courage to stand up against peer pressure...*

Maybe you know there is something physically wrong in your body, but you're afraid to go to the doctor? You're afraid of what they may tell you? But you must make up your mind and be strong and courageous. It's time to trust God no matter what kind of report you get. Go ahead and make that appointment with the doctor. Go ahead and trust God with courage believing that God can help you. Courage means you will no longer let fear hold you back.

Because peer pressure can be relentless, we frequently feel a pull toward doing things that we know are wrong. It takes enormous courage to stand up against peer pressure, so we have to make up our minds up in advance that we're going to do the right thing. If you will put God first, He will command the blessing on you.

Perhaps you know that you're dating someone that is not good for you. But you don't have the courage to walk away because you're afraid of being alone. You must make up your mind to keep walking by faith and trusting in Him whatever you are going through. Trust Him even if you are going to be alone for a while, because God is able to work that out to your good. You must believe that if you step out in faith and do the right thing, God will help you.

> *God wants you to know that you can do all things through Christ who strengthens you. He wants you to know that you are more than a conqueror*

God wants you to know that you can do all things through Christ who strengthens you. He wants you to know that you are more than a conqueror through Christ Jesus, not in yourself, but through Christ Jesus who loves you.

Some years ago the Lord spoke to me about overcoming all the fears in my life. I began to confront each one that I knew of, and afterwards, even fears that I didn't know were there. Then God began to strengthen me. Let me tell you, it is so exhilarating when you begin to conquer a fear that has held you back for years. There's something that will happen inside your heart when you begin to conquer the fear, the very thing that has been holding you back. Courage is nothing more than facing fears and trusting God to help you.

I don't have to feel faith to speak faith. I don't have to feel faith to walk in faith, but when my courage is under fire, that's when I have to be the most determined to speak faith and to walk in faith.

One of the most common reasons Christians don't succeed is fear. But when you are strong and courageous God will bring success your way. Job said, "the thing I feared most has come upon me." Job loved the Lord, but he had a constant fear of losing everything he had until one day he did. People who walk in constant fear are people who always fail. Anytime someone is afraid of failure they always find a way to fail. When someone is afraid to be alone they pull people to them so tightly they suffocate them, and they drain the life out of the people they love and need. Then they are lonelier than ever, and the cycle repeats itself.

One of the most common reasons Christians don't succeed is fear.

If you're always afraid that you'll get hurt, you will get hurt. If you're always afraid of failing, you will always fail. The surest way to live under a spirit of failure is through fear. What are you afraid of today? What is intimidating you? I know people that were so afraid of cancer they eventually got cancer. I'm telling you, *fear opens the door for the enemy to come in.* Fear says that nothing is going to work out in your life. But stand firm and say, "My God has everything under control. He's working all things together for my good. It may not look good today, but my God is working all things for my good."

> *Anytime you are greatly discouraged, it's nothing more than the spirit of fear that makes you believe that things aren't going to work out.*

Anytime you are greatly discouraged, it's nothing more than the spirit of fear that makes you believe that things aren't going to work out. Your faith in God's loving protection is gone. The enemy has stolen your courage. You must tell discouragement, "No way, Jose." The next time fear knocks, you need courage to go to the door. You can't help it if fear comes along, but you can control the way you respond. You can be courageous, you can walk in faith, and you can trust God.

Fear does not go away by ignoring it. You will always be afraid of the water unless you have the courage to take swimming lessons. You will always be afraid of people that are a different color than you unless you make up your mind to make changes. Take somebody out to lunch that is a different color than you, and put your arms around somebody that's a different color than you and say, "I will not be afraid." The devil's plan is for you to be afraid of white people. He wants you to be afraid of black folk or brown folk or yellow or red or whatever. If you have a problem with a particular color, you must do something about it or that fear will control you all of your life.

> *When the disciples saw Jesus walking on the water they became frightened and thought He was a ghost. In their fear Jesus said, "Take courage."*

When the disciples saw Jesus walking on the water they became frightened and thought He was a ghost. In their fear Jesus said, "Take courage." That's what you have to do. In your fear, you have to take courage. Whatever comes against you in your fear, you must make up your mind to take courage.

In the Parable of the Talents the one who had one talent, one measure of money, did nothing with it because he was afraid of losing it. Then God took away what he had. That's what fear will do to you; it will cause you to lose what you already have. The number one reason people don't tithe is because they're afraid they won't have enough money. They're afraid God won't help them, and because of fear they end up living under a financial curse all of their life. That's why I'm always trying to encourage you to make a covenant with God, because He's already promised in the covenant to bless you. There is something about fear that keeps you from being blessed.

There's something about fear that causes you to live under a spirit of failure. Be courageous. Your words either promote faith or your words promote fear. That's why you have to be careful of the things you say. "Death and life are in the power of the tongue" (Proverbs 18:21). The tongue is like a rudder of a ship that will guide you to safety or guide you to destruction. Your words are like a bit in a horse's mouth that will guide you to the finish line or cause you to crash and burn. As long as you speak fear out of your mouth, that's

> *There's something about fear that causes you to live under a spirit of failure. Be courageous.*

all you'll ever have. "I'm afraid to pay my tithes. I'm afraid to get into another relationship. I'm afraid to build my own business." The devil is a liar because God has not given you a spirit of fear.

Moses wrote, "I will say of the Lord, He is my refuge . . . Him will I trust" (Psalm 91:2). You have to say what God would have you say, not what fear will have you say. Psalm 91:7-12 tells us that even if "A thousand fall at my side and ten thousand at my right hand . . . There shall no evil befall me . . . For He has given His angels charge over me to guard me in all my ways, and to bear me up in their hands lest I dash my foot against a stone."

Faith isn't a feeling. It's putting action together. Let me tell you what God says about your situation. "The Lord is my light and my salvation: whom shall I fear? The Lord is the strength of my life; of whom shall I be afraid?" (Psalm 27:1). I will not fear what man can do to me. You need to be like David and talk to your giants. "You come at me with a bad report, but I tell you, you're coming down today. I come at you in the Name of the Lord."

> *You need to talk to your fears, talk to your sickness, talk to your family problems, and talk to your poverty...*

You need to talk to your fears, talk to your sickness, talk to your family problems, and talk to your poverty. David said in Psalm 23, "The Lord is my shepherd; I shall not want. He maketh me to lie down in green pastures: he leadeth me beside the still waters. He restoreth my soul." I'm so glad I serve a God of restoration. He's bringing everything back that I lost. I'm putting God first, and He will give me double for my trouble and triple for the ripple.

God did it for Job, and He's going to do it for me. David

said again in Psalm 23, "Yea, though I walk through the valley of the shadow of death, I will fear no evil: for thou art with me." I'm talking about speaking faith out of your mouth. Making up your mind to throw your shoulders back, lift your head up high, be strong and courageous. I'm talking about speaking faith out of your mouth. Fear says nothing is going to work out, but faith says, "No weapon formed against me shall prosper" (Isaiah 54:17).

When it looks like I can't make it, I put on courage. Make up your mind to trust in God. You may be in the fiery furnace, but the Lord is with you. You may be in the lion's den, but the Lord is with you. The Bible says that the devil, your adversary, walks about like a roaring lion seeking whom he may devour, but resist him by standing firm in your faith. You need to know that the devil can't devour everybody. So he's looking for somebody who's walking in fear. He's looking for somebody who's timid. He's looking for somebody who won't step out in faith and that's why you must be determined that fear is not going to control you. Without faith, it's impossible to please God, but without fear, it's impossible to please the devil. That's why I am determined that fear will no longer control me.

Even when fear comes crashing against your mind, resist it firmly in your faith. Take courage, and refuse to let the devil cause you to back up, don't let him shut you up. Keep your mouth going and keep speaking faith.

Philippians 4:5 says, "Be anxious for nothing, but in everything by prayer and supplication with thanksgiving, let your requests be made known unto God." It's all in God's hands. I've been praying, and I've been trusting in God, and it's all in His hands.

> *If I had given into that fear, this ministry would not exist today. It's time to deal with all of the fears in your life.*

In the early days I was a businessman, and I was afraid to step out in ministry because I was afraid I was going to be broke all my life. Fear nearly kept me from stepping out and starting Heritage Christian Center. If I had given into that fear, this ministry would not exist today. It's time to deal with all of the fears in your life.

I want to take a minute and encourage you right now. I rebuke every generational curse in your life with Jesus' name. I rebuke the spirit of fear over your life with Jesus' name. It's time to lay hands on your head and tell the devil "God has not given me a spirit of fear, but of power and of love and of a sound mind." It's time for you to give up all the leftovers and to into the promises of God.

6

WALKING ON EGG SHELLS

The writer of Hebrews said that we have to lay aside all the weight, all the hindrances, all the encumbrances that would keep us from fulfilling what God has called us to do. If you are super sensitive, you will never fulfill your purpose because you will quit too soon. Things will hurt you too deeply, and you won't be able to go on. If you are tired of leftovers and hand-me-downs in your life, you need to lay aside all your super sensitivity and always put God first.

People who are extremely sensitive are people who carry tremendous pain from their past. They have issues inside that must be faced. If there is any chance that you might be a super-sensitive person, you have to take the mask off. You have to be willing to say, "Yes, I am a little bit too sensitive." Until you can confess your faults, you can't overcome them. As Christians we're called to confess our faults to one another so that we may be healed, yet being that open is really tough for a super-sensitive person.

> ...the super-sensitive person is super sensitive for a reason. They weren't just born that way; it comes from the wounding and the scarring from abuse, manipulation, or extreme control in their past.

But remember, the super-sensitive person is super sensitive for a reason. They weren't just born that way; it comes from the wounding and the scarring from abuse, manipulation, or extreme control in their past. Overly sensitive people have reached out for love but usually received the opposite and were left feeling misused and victimized. They were criticized; they were beaten down, and told they would never amount to anything. Super-sensitive persons were usually raised by a parent who was impossible to please, for whom nothing was ever good enough. The by-product of this harsh past is super sensitivity.

If people have to walk on eggshells around you, you probably have very few friends. The problem with sensitive people is that you have to be careful with every word you say. When they get hurt, sensitive people should say, "You hurt me," but instead, they say by their words or actions, "I need my space." The truth is, they don't need space. They've been hurt, and they are trying to get away from you to keep you from hurting them again.

And of course, some people who are super sensitive, just blow up. Then there is the other type of the super-sensitive person that just gives you the silent treatment. Yet just because they don't lose their temper and choose to go the silent way, doesn't mean that they're right.

> *If you were not encouraged to be all you could be as a child, then you may have grown up to be a low achiever.*

If you were not encouraged to be all you could be as a child, then you may have grown up to be a low achiever. If your parents were critical of you or told you that you were no good, then you are probably super sensitive. Now, we all have wounds from the past that need to be healed, and we all have scars that make us sensitive. But, if you fall into the category of a super-sensitive person, and if you don't learn to overcome the work of the flesh, you will probably live under a spirit of failure all of your life. It's time to overcome every work of the flesh so that you can eat the fruit of the land.

There is the pain of watching your parents fighting. There is the pain of being rejected by people in your family, or friends that should have loved you. As a result, you've become super sensitive, and now people have to walk on eggshells when they are around you. But God wants each of us to set aside the hindrances and come to Him, He wants us to know who we are in Christ. We're somebody, we're a royal priesthood, and we are more than conquerors through Him (Romans 8:37). He is healing us and we are becoming victorious in our walk with Him, but we have to take the masks off.

> *We have to begin to seek Him for healing. We have to be able to confess who and what we really are.*

We have to begin to seek Him for healing. We have to be able to confess who and what we really are. You may have so many bad memories that you don't even want to think about it. You don't want to talk about the past because it's too painful, but if you are going to receive healing, you have to face yourself, face your past, and confess your weaknesses. The worst thing you can do is try to cover it up.

Unfortunately, if you are overly sensitive, people will keep their distance from you because they've already learned their lesson. Many times people will say, "Oh, Bishop, pray for me." But the problem is not the devil. The problem is their flesh. Because of their sensitivity, they are running from things that are not chasing them. They think that folk are talking about them, when they could care less about them. They think that folk are plotting against them.

> *The person with low self-esteem needs constant reassurance. It's time to lay aside all of the low self esteem and believe God for all of His promises.*

Overly sensitive people need a whole lot of approval. In fact, they need so much approval that you could tell them you love them every ten minutes, and they'll say, "No, you don't." "Oh, I love you baby!" "No, you don't." No matter how much love you try to give them, it is never quite enough.

The warfare is in their own flesh. The warfare is in their own mind. Overly sensitive people almost always have low self esteem, and the person with low self esteem is always self centered. I don't mean they are selfish, I mean they are always wondering why are people against them? They are always wondering why nothing ever works out for them? The person with low self-esteem needs constant reassurance. It's time to lay aside all of the low self esteem and believe God for all of His promises.

Depression is something that almost always attacks the

overly sensitive person. That's why we need to be able to admit these issues in our lives and go to the root cause. You see there is a root cause for every emotional issue that we have in our lives. We're a product of all the things that we've been exposed to. We're a product of the experiences that we've had, but also a product of the way we were raised and the way we were treated.

> *Many times it's our guilt complex that make us think that God is mad at us. But our guilt complex is often nothing more than the voices of our parents from times past.*

Many times we feel guilty, because we think that God is mad at us. Many times it's our guilt complex that make us think that God is mad at us. But our guilt complex is often nothing more than the voices of our parents from times past. God is not mad at us, but many times we are haunted by the fact that our parents were difficult to please. Any time a parent is too hard to please, depression can take root in your life. If your parents made you believe that you didn't measure up, then you may struggle with being overly sensitive and with depression.

When parents try to control a child with guilt, that child will live with guilty feelings for a lifetime. Sometimes I give messages on submission to authority, but let me tell you, if you were raised by parents that controlled through guilt all the time, you can't receive the message on submission to authority.

If you were raised by parents that tried to control you with guilt, it can even be difficult to step foot inside a church. There are people reading this book, who were raised under a spirit of guilt and who equate guilt with God. Now, no one wants to go to church if they think it's all about control and guilt. But I'm telling you, God isn't mad at you; God loves you, and He has a plan for you. If you struggle in this area, then you have to get into the right kind of church where you know that God's love is true.

> *The Holy Spirit convicts you of your sin so that you will turn from your sin. The devil, on the other hand, uses guilt to hurt you, hold you down, and condemn you.*

The Holy Spirit convicts you of your sin so that you will turn from your sin. The devil, on the other hand, uses guilt to hurt you, hold you down, and condemn you. That's the difference between what the Lord does and what the devil does. The Holy Ghost will simply convict you so you will come to the Lord. Guilt can be good, if it causes you to repent. But usually guilt doesn't cause you to repent, it causes you to stay away from church, to forget about the things of

God, and to put your Bible down and say, "Oh, forget it."

Anytime you have a friendship with an overly sensitive person, they can be a whole lot of work. I call them high-maintenance friends; that is, they require so much attention it will drain the life out of you. And if you don't give them all that they need, they will get their feelings hurt. In fact, they may even turn on you before it's over.

> People who are emotionally sensitive and easily hurt have a tendency to take what people say far too personally.

People who are emotionally sensitive and easily hurt have a tendency to take what people say far too personally. But the highly sensitive person focuses too much on their own pain, and they tend to live in a pity party all the time. "Woe is me. Nobody's got a husband as bad as mine. Nobody's got a job situation as bad as mine," and they live under a spirit of failure all of their lives. It's time to give God all of your hurts so that you can fulfill your purpose and destiny.

Overly sensitive people concentrate on their own needs so much that they are self-centered. And because they are self-centered, they are always looking at what they can get out of a relationship rather than what they can put into a relationship. You see, when someone is healthy emotionally, they direct their emotions outwardly. A healthy person knows that happiness comes by giving and not by receiving. And because of that, they concentrate on serving in the church. They concentrate on serving their family.

> *The flesh is self-centered. The flesh loves to wallow in self-pity. Some folk don't even want help because they love their self-pity too much.*

Sensitive people care too much about themselves and not enough about others. If you want to see the healing process begin in your life, you have to start by giving. You always keep what you give away. You always lose what you hang onto. If you will focus on blessing others and the things of God, you will find your sensitivity begin to change because you will begin to get the focus off of yourself. Focusing on you is the problem.

The flesh is self-centered. The flesh loves to wallow in self-pity. Some folk don't even want help because they love their self-pity too much. Overly sensitive people are so self-centered they make very few sacrifices. They are more concerned with what they can get rather than what they can give. The reason some folk aren't involved in the church is because they are trying to get their healing, when their healing comes by giving. A healthy person is a giver.

Any time your thoughts and intentions are directed at blessing other people, you will barely notice when other folk give you a dirty look. I said we barely notice. We saw it, but we didn't let it get inside of us. I don't know about you, but I'm tired of the pity parties. I'm ready to be blessed by the Lord.

> You have to begin to look within yourself. You may have to go back years, I don't know. But at some point you have to say, "Oh, I know why I'm dragging this baggage around.

Many times sensitive people cover up their sensitivity by just being loud and obnoxious. Do you know any loud and obnoxious people? Many times super-sensitive folk cover it up by being hard on the outside. They may even be abusive in order to cover up their sensitivity. You'll find sensitive people have a difficult time forgiving others. In fact, they frequently want to get even because they've been hurt so deeply themselves. They are not known for flexibility and always want to have their own way. "Well, I need to take care of my hurts you know. We have to do it my way because I deserve it; I have been hurt you know.

You have to begin to look within yourself. You may have to go back years, I don't know. But at some point you have to say, "Oh, I know why I'm dragging this baggage around. I know how that got into my life. I see it and now I forgive the people that did that to me. I'm going to let it go, but God, I know that unless you help me it's not going to change." At some point you have to get a hold of God. Get a hold of the horns of the altar and say, "God, I give you this weak part of my life." You have to face your past and get it under the Blood. Forgive everybody, and say, "I'm starting a new life right now!" The healing process begins the moment you admit you have an issue. There are so many things that wound us. If you were raised by parents that never kept their promises, then you are probably overly sensitive today when people don't do what they say they are going to do.

If you're married, you need to be able to say, "Baby, I have this weakness, and this is why it's here. I need your strength, and I need your support. Because this happened in my past, I have some trust issues in this area, and I need you to help me."

> *If you're married, you need to be able to say, "Baby, I have this weakness, and this is why it's here. I need your strength, and I need your support.*

You have to humble yourself if you expect God to raise you up. But now that you are born again, you can begin the process of taking care of your baggage and eventually eliminating it. Maybe your issues were unforgiveness, pride, or jealousy. As you see your issues, set them aside and work on them. They've been holding you under a spirit of failure for too long. Healing may not come overnight, but it will come. You may be living with leftovers, but God is going to turn it around.

Jesus came to bind up all your brokenness, to bring healing into your life. Maybe you're overly sensitive today, but you are working on it, and now you are responsible for your own actions. You can't help where you've been, but you can help where you are going. That's why you've got to stop blaming everyone else for your problems. Maybe you were a victim BC (before Christ), but now you are more than a conqueror through Christ Jesus who gave His life for you and loves you.

> *Jesus came to bind up all your brokenness, to bring healing into your life.*

You'll never build a fantastic marriage, a great family, a wonderful business, or an incredible ministry until you lay aside all the sensitive areas of your life. It's time to stop blaming everybody else, and take the mask off. It's time to quit pretending that you are okay. Because Jesus said, "You will know them by their fruit" (Matt. 7:16). You can tell by the fruit in your life whether or not you are okay. It's time to get your past behind you, and it's time to change. It's time to put God first and watch Him bless you.

What are your issues? The woman with the issue of blood pressed through to touch the Master. What is your issue? Maybe it's depression. You have to get to the root of that depression. There is a reason you're depressed. Quit acting like you are okay. Maybe it's super sensitivity? It's time to go to the Lord and ask for His healing.

If you go from church to church, and you have problems everywhere you go, then maybe it's not the churches, it's you. It's always good to have faith, but sometimes you have to deal with your issue. You can keep binding the devil all day long, but if you're the problem, it won't help much.

Lay aside every weight, every impediment, and every hindrance. "Oh, I don't have an issue." Well, your pride has you deceived. It is so hard for us to admit weakness because we've been taught not to. But before you will ever see a great change in your life, you need to face your issues of pride and admit; "I've got a problem. I've got an issue." Then make up your mind and say, "God, I need your help I can't do it without you." If you're willing and obedient, you will have God's best.

7

OVERCOMING FAILURE THROUGH PRAYER

When we examine the original Hebrew scriptures, we see that God gave us images of things that were to come in the renewed covenant. God did away with the law when Jesus went to the cross, but not the promises in the original covenant. Therefore, the Old Testament is still relevant for today.

We have blessings stored up for us by obeying the Word of God, whether it's the Old Covenant or the New Covenant. God always gave us images, and one place we find them is in the tabernacle. One of those images was the prayer shawl. First of all, the Word of God is very clear on how the prayer shawl should be made, because every detail God relates to us has significance. He directs the Israelites to make the prayer shawl out of a certain material for specific reasons. Typically the Israelites were supposed to pray with their prayer shawl at least three times a day. We ought to pray without ceasing.

He put blue threads in the corners so that every time you look at the prayer shawl, you will remember the commandments of the Lord. You will remember that if you obey all that God has told you to do, you will be blessed, highly favored, and empowered to prosper.

> *So as we think about prayer, it's a picture to remind us of God and His Word.*

So as we think about prayer, it's a picture to remind us of God and His Word. We don't necessarily have to use a prayer shawl, but let me tell you, it is a great reminder. It reminds us not only to pray three times a day, but when you look at the blue thread, you'll think, "Wait a minute, God made me a promise that if I will obey all that He has commanded me, He'll command the blessing on me wherever I go."

From the very beginning of time God created man in order to have a relationship with Him. That is what prayer is all about. It's an aid to remind us of our relationship with Him. We are not going to go to heaven because we pray three times a day. We're going to go to heaven because our faith is in Jesus the Messiah.

When God created Adam, and Adam began to pray, the way was opened for man to relate to God through prayer. Finite man had the infinite God as Friend, Advisor, and Partner. God could answer man and guide him through prayer. That's what God wants to do with you today. He wants to be in partnership with you. We go to church not just to pray, but also to be in relationship with the Lord.

Isaiah built an altar and then he prayed. It's about a partnership. Jacob built an altar. He would simply begin to pray. It's a remembrance of the Lord. You may say, "Wait a minute I can't get this done by myself, but I'm in partnership with God. I'm in partnership with Hashem. I'm in relationship with Jehovah God. He is my God, I am one of His children."

> *Isaiah built an altar and then he prayed. It's about a partnership. Jacob built an altar. He would simply begin to pray. It's a remembrance of the Lord.*

People who don't pray are people who think they can get things done by themselves. That's not what God wants us to do. He wants to provide for our needs, but He's looking for individuals who will come into relationship with Him.

When it appeared that Rachel would never have children, she was devastated. In fact, she wanted children so badly she said, "Give me children, or I will die." Have you ever wanted something so badly in your life that you said, "God, I'll die if I don't get it."

> *Year after year, Rachel would cry out to the Lord for a miracle. Year after year, she would pray for God to give her children, and she made up her mind not to quit.*

Year after year, Rachel would cry out to the Lord for a miracle. Year after year, she would pray for God to give her children, and she made up her mind not to quit. She was absolutely determined to get a hold of God. That's what you have to understand, you have to be absolutely determined. If you don't get it this year, you're not going to quit praying next year.

The Bible says that the Lord remembered her prayers. Are you willing to seek God year after year to get what you are believing for? Are you willing to cry out to God for years with tears running down your face? Are you willing to be in church whenever the doors are open or are you slipping in 45 minutes late then sneaking out early?

Are you willing to do whatever you have to do to see the doors open in your life? Are you willing to do all that He has commanded you in the Word in order to see that happen in your life? Are you willing to place yourself under the authority of the Word of God in order to have what you're believing God for in your life? Are you willing to put God first in every area of your life and wait for Him to bless you?

> *The Bible says that Jacob had to wrestle with God all night long. He said, "God, I'm not going to let go of you until you bless me."*

The Bible says that Jacob had to wrestle with God all night long. He said, "God, I'm not going to let go of you until you bless me." Are you willing to wrestle with God until something changes? Are you willing to cry out to Him until something moves in your life? Are you willing to fight the good fight in prayer? Are you willing to let the devil know he can't have your family? Are you willing to let God know you're not going to let go of Him until you're blessed?

Paul said, "We wrestle not with flesh and blood, but principalities and powers and rulers of darkness in high places" (Ephesians 6:12). It's your spiritual enemy trying to hinder your prayers. Anytime you're praying for God to change something, you can bet that your spiritual enemy has heard your prayers and is trying to run interference against you.

Your spiritual enemy will do everything he can to hinder

God's plan in your life just like static on a radio. The radio is still working, but something is disrupting the signal. But if you'll keep working and keep your dial on the station, eventually it will clear up. The same thing is true in your prayer life. When you start praying, the enemy brings all kinds of static against the things you're praying for, but if you'll continue calling out to God, everything will begin to clear up.

> If you have some battles in your life today, you have to make up your mind to fight the good fight of faith.

If you have some battles in your life today, you have to make up your mind to fight the good fight of faith. You have to make up your mind to get back to prayer like you used to pray. The church needs mothers who will gather around the altar before every service. We need fathers who will walk the aisles and pray the Blood of Jesus over the church and its families. Quit waiting for somebody to rally you to prayer. You have to make up your mind that you are going to be a man or a woman of prayer.

You have to understand that God put all authority in the hands of the church, and God does nothing unless we pray and partner with Him. Yes, He is God, but you have to partner with Him or He doesn't do anything. Read chapter 1 of Ephesians. God put the authority in the hands of the church. You don't have to put up with the devil's mess in your life. You don't have to put up with the devil's mess in your house.

When King Herod began to persecute those who were preaching the gospel of Jesus Christ, he seized Peter and put him in prison (Acts12). The king placed soldiers all around him and had guards chained to Peter because he didn't want to take any chances of Peter getting loose. But they didn't know the church was praying. The odds were against Peter, but the church was praying. He was greatly outnumbered, but the church was

> *Those wimpy prayers have got to go. You have to quit praying, "Oh Lord, please bless them." You have to say, "Devil, get back on your side of the line.*

praying. I don't know what you're going through today, but if you'll get some prayer partners and begin to partner with God, I'm telling you the devil can't hold on to that thing for very long.

The Bible says that the church prayed fervently for Peter. They were praying hot prayers for Peter. You see, when you need a miracle, you have to quit praying those namby-pamby prayers. Those wimpy prayers have got to go. You have to quit praying, "Oh Lord, please bless them." You have to say, "Devil, get back on your side of the line. I take authority over you in the Name of Jesus."

Anytime you're praying a prayer of consecration like Jesus did in the garden, you can pray, "Lord, if it be Thy will." But when you've already got God's Word for healing, you don't say, "If it be Your will." You say, "I know what Your will is and I stand on the Word."

You know that the god of this world, the devil, has blinded the eyes of the unbelieving. That's why, when you are praying for your family members to get saved, you have to command those blinders to come off in the name of Jesus. Pray, "God, break the devil's powers of deception in their lives; open their eyes to see the truth, and open their hearts to receive it. And may I say, people don't get saved unless somebody is praying.

God is looking for people who will partner with Him in prayer.

God is looking for people who will partner with Him in prayer. He has limited Himself in many ways to the reach of our prayers. He wants us as partners who will pray with Him. He gave us the authority through the church, and He can do anything if we will just pray. You see, you can be a good person, but nothing is going to happen until you make up your mind to pray. Some things do not change unless we pray.

Let me say to every husband: You need to be praying with your wife. I know you are busy making a living, and I know that you don't want her to know how you pray, if you pray at all, but God has called you to lead your house. He's called you to lead your family, and He's called you to partner with your wife, and the two of you to partner with Him. "Where any two agree as touching anything, it shall be done for them" (Matt. 18:19).

> *Let me say to every husband...God has called you to lead your house. He's called you to lead your family, and He's called you to partner with your wife*

It looked like Peter's life was over. Yes, it looked like everything was finished, but the church began to pray the chains off of Peter. No wonder the devil doesn't want you to pray. I'm telling you that no matter what the odds may look like against you, if you'll pray, things will change. Prayer changes things. "Be anxious for nothing, but in everything by prayer and supplication with thanksgiving let your requests be made known unto God" (Philippians 4:6). God is looking for somebody who will partner with Him in prayer.

I'm talking about having a relationship and trusting God in prayer. I'm talking about leaning on the Lord in prayer. "Those that wait on Him shall renew their strength" (Isaiah 40:31). There's nothing the devil dreads more than a praying

No More Leftovers

Christian. Satan laughs at our programs, but he trembles when we pray. No wonder the devil fights you so hard in prayer. No wonder you are too busy to pray.

God told Moses that the people should make themselves prayer shawls. It's a picture to show that you have got to cover everything you do in prayer. Too often what we do is pray, "God, bless my plans," when we ought to be praying, "God, what are your plans?" And we are so busy praying, we don't have time to listen. We pray, "God, I've got three minutes. Hang on, I'm going to get this in." But we ought to pray and wait. Pray and listen. We need to pray and be quiet.

> *God told Moses that the people should make themselves prayer shawls. It's a picture to show that you have got to cover everything you do in prayer.*

"Be still and know that I am God" (Psalm 46:10). Pray, "God, what are you telling me? Now I'm obeying all that I know, but I must not be obeying everything, so tell me where am I missing it? Show me how to obey Your Word and be under authority."

The tabernacle was relatively small. Very few people could get inside at one time. Those who could not make it inside the tabernacle would gather around outside, take their

-101-

prayer shawls, and have church right there. You don't have to be in church to pray. You can pray in your car, pray at work, or pray in the bathroom.

Everything has to be covered in prayer. Rivers do not part without prayer. Mountains do not move without prayer. Families don't change without prayer. Breakthroughs do not happen without prayer. Miracles do not come without prayer.

"If my people, which are called by my name, shall humble themselves, and pray, and seek my face, and turn from their wicked ways; then I will hear from heaven, and will forgive their sin, and will heal their land" (2 Chronicles 7:14). What a promise! God will hear from heaven, He'll forgive us, and He'll heal our land. If we'll pray, He will heal our families.

> Jesus said, "Whatever you ask for in my name, my Father will do it" (John 16:13).

Jesus said, "Whatever you ask for in my name, my Father will do it" (John 16:13). There is a key to unlocking heaven's gates. It's the name of Jesus. I don't mean to offend anybody, but it's not the name of Mohammed. I've never prayed in the name of Mohammed, but I can tell you I've prayed in the name of Jesus. And I can tell you things happen when you pray in Jesus' name. Now I've never prayed in the name of

Buddha, but I can tell you things change when you pray in Jesus' name. There is a name that's above every name and at the name of Jesus every knee shall bow and every tongue shall confess that Jesus is Lord of all (Philippians 2:9,10).

> The Word says that we always ought to pray and to faint not (Luke 18:1). Jesus said, "ask and keep on asking, seek and keep on seeking, knock and keep on knocking" (Matthew 7:7,8).

Do you realize that no devil can stand up to the name of Jesus? He disarmed the devil. He made a public display of him. James said that demons tremble at the mention of His name.

The Word says that we always ought to pray and to faint not (Luke 18:1). Jesus said, "ask and keep on asking, seek and keep on seeking, knock and keep on knocking" (Matthew 7:7,8). That's what we're going to do. We're going to pray and we're going to knock and we're going to seek and we're going to keep on asking because things do not change unless somebody prays. Doors don't open unless somebody prays.

When you are praying for your family to get saved, God sends out His army. Your friends can be in a nightclub sipping a drink, and when you are praying, the Holy Ghost moves in and sits on the stool right next to them. Then He whispers in your friend's ear, "You're better than this. You don't belong in here. Put that drink down, and let's get out of here." I'm telling you, as long as you will pray, the Holy Ghost will dog their tracks. They can run, but they can't hide. They can change their name, but the Holy Ghost will track them down.

If you are unsaved or if you are a Christian in rebellion and somebody is praying fervently for you, you might as well surrender now. That's because, when people are praying for those trapped by sin, the Holy Ghost can take all the fun right out of that sin. He can ruin the whole thing. They may still sin, but they won't enjoy it. Then finally one day they'll just stand up and say, "I don't know why I'm doing this, I'm through with it."

Let me tell you, the only reason I'm here today is because my mom and dad wouldn't give up on me. I tried to go to hell, but they prayed me back to Jesus. I'm trying to tell you that God's way is for us to pray. "Pray ye for one another so that you may be healed" (James 5:16).

Daniel fasted and prayed for twenty-one days, and God sent his answer. Daniel said, "God, why did you take so long?" God said, "I heard your prayers the very first day you prayed, but the enemy also heard them, and he hindered your prayers for twenty straight days. But because you were persistent, on the twenty-first day my angels were able to break through that line of defense."

So many times we do not receive answers to prayer because we quit on the twentieth day. If we had just been a little more persistent, we could have received the answers.

> *...we need to persist and follow through even if our inclination is to give up. In any kind of spiritual warfare, you must fight with spiritual weapons and prayer must under gird everything.*

We need to be persistent, but we also need to follow through. Lack of persistence and follow-through can lead to big-time trouble in our homes, marriages, businesses, and ministries.

Listen, the older I get, the less I like to fight. But we need to persist and follow through even if our inclination is to give up. In any kind of spiritual warfare, you must fight with spiritual weapons and prayer must under gird everything. Since the powers and principalities battling against us are much more powerful and intelligent than we are, we will lose every confrontation if we don't fight according to the principles set forth in the Scriptures. And the primary weapon is prayer. You must learn to fight the good fight of faith through prayer so that you can have God's best in your life. If you are willing and obedient, you will eat the good of the land.

8

REVERSE THE CURSE

Every single day you have choices to make in your life. God has set before you the blessing and the curse, and every single day you must make the decision whether you are walking under the blessing or walking under the curse.

That is why the devil is trying so hard to get people back in the drug scene. He is trying to get them to bring a curse on themselves. You see, when you walk under the blessing and you chose to do it God's way, you'll have joy and you'll have peace. You may not have all the money yet, but you'll have happiness. If you only knew that serving God with all your heart would bring you happiness unlike anything you've ever experienced in your life, you would quit holding onto that sin that you think you like so well.

When you walk under the blessing, you'll walk in prosperity. You'll walk in love. You'll walk in health. You'll walk in generational blessings. There's always a price to pay for generational blessings. But in my own case, in all the days I can remember, my father served God. He wasn't a perfect man, but none of us are. But he always taught me to put God first, to tithe, and to give offerings above the tithe.

I can remember so many times when I was growing up how my dad would be trusting God in his own business. I can remember how he and mom would gather together and write a check and plant seed saying, "We're believing God in our lives."

> I can remember so many times when I was growing up how my dad would be trusting God in his own business. I can remember how he and mom would gather together and write a check and plant seed saying, "We're believing God in our lives."

Then he passed that generational blessing along to me. Even when I wasn't serving God, even when I didn't know if there was a God, I was still blessed because of the blessing that was passed to me through him.

Now, I can pass along that same blessing to my sons, and even though they aren't perfect either, they are blessed because the blessing came from their grandfather, through me to them. The blessing is a wonderful, beneficial thing even if there are times when we don't deserve to be blessed. Its benefits are still there. And as long as my sons makes up their minds to serve God, that same blessing is going to be passed down to the next generation.

When I'm walking in the blessing there is life and joy, peace, happiness, growth, and productivity. Everything I touch is blessed. When I'm walking under the blessing of God I'm obeying Him, I'm putting Him first. All I have to do is the right thing.

Life can be so hard anyway, but it can be made even harder by unwise choices. Recently my wife

> *Life can be so hard anyway, but it can be made even harder by unwise choices.*

was ministering in a prison. She explained how sad it was to think that many of those people were badly influenced because of a generational curse that started with their grandparents and went down to their parents and then were passed right on to them. With the Lord and a lot of prayer, they can begin to break free of the generational curse, but it's not easy and they need our support. If the curse isn't broken, it will pass on down to another generation.

Maybe you don't care if you walk under the blessing or not? Maybe your heart is so hard that you don't care if you lose everything you have? But think of your children and grandchildren; surely you don't want to pass the same curse onto them and leave them struggling under that burden?

When you're walking under the curse, there is bitterness and hatred and depression. Everything you touch seems to fall apart. Everything you touch seems to fail. Remember, if you're redeemed from the curse, you're redeemed from poverty and sickness. I don't mean to say that if you are a Christian you won't have sickness because in the natural course of life you might struggle with sickness in your body. Just living in a world that is under a curse means you might struggle with sicknesses in this life.

> *Nobody can curse what God has blessed. If you chose to obey God, you'll end up walking in the blessing. If you chose to disobey God, you'll walk under the curse...*

Nobody can curse what God has blessed. If you chose to obey God, you'll end up walking in the blessing. If you chose to disobey God, you'll walk under the curse—and I don't care how close you are to your minister or any other spiritual leader. So, maybe you just need to tell the devil, "Hey, devil, I've changed my mind! I've decided I'm going to be blessed."

When we tithe, we are saying we are determined to walk out from underneath the curse. That's all tithing is about, "I will not be cursed." The children of Israel were always falling under a curse because they served God one day and did their own thing the next day. One day they worshiped God, but the next day they worshiped a golden calf.

The Christian who worships Jesus Christ one day and trusts in the horoscope the next day is in danger of falling under the curse. Christians who go to church on Sunday and call the psychic hotline on Friday night are destined to live under a spirit of failure because they are trusting in a god other than the most High God.

> *The Christian who worships Jesus Christ one day and trusts in the horoscope the next day is in danger of falling under the curse.*

If you study the Bible, you will see that God always allowed a famine wherever His people did not put Him first. Death always followed God's people when they would not put Him first. When the children of Israel fell into idolatry, God allowed them to go into slavery. Anytime people let anything come between them and God, they are in danger of dreadful judgments like famine, slavery, captivity, and death.

God created sexuality for a good thing. But if you live outside of God's will, you will find yourself in slavery. Drugs open up your mind to the demonic realm and can lead you into slavery. Again, anything that comes between you and

God can bring a curse on you. But listen to this, the curse will not only hit you but will fall upon your children and your grandchildren. God said a good man leaves an inheritance to his children and his children's children (Psalm 3:22). What kind of an inheritance are you leaving to your children? What kind of an inheritance are you leaving to your grandchildren? Are you leaving them a curse or a Godly inheritance?

> God said a good man leaves an inheritance to his children and his children's childre n (Ps. 13:22). What kind of an inheritance are you leaving to your children?

If you love God, and you are a smoker, you're in slavery. Don't get mad at me. I'm just giving you the Word of God. I'm just the delivery boy here. I didn't say you weren't going to heaven. I said you are in slavery because of your addiction.

Certainly I don't have to tell you that you can't have any statues of Buddha in your home, or that following a new age guru will cause you to miss God's best. Surely I don't have to tell you that wearing occult or zodiac jewelry or using ouiji boards, fortune-tellers, and tarot cards can bring you under a curse. But, if you repent and repudiate your involvement, and then destroy these items, you can reverse the curse today.

Cases in point are the battles of Jericho and Ai in which fallen human nature brings defeat and death shortly after a miraculous victory at Jericho. When God brought the children of Israel near the city of Jericho, He told them that they would be able to take the city. The city looked invincible. But the Lord promised victory if they would do exactly what He said. That's what God is trying to tell you right now. If you would obey Him, He'll work everything out.

Even though the city was a mighty fortress, and even though the children of Israel were greatly outnumbered, God fought their battle for them, and they defeated Jericho. Even though the odds were against them, God caused them to win. When you are blessed from the Lord, God will eventually cause you to win in your situation.

After defeating Jericho, the children of Israel were on their way to Jerusalem, when they came upon a little city by the name of Ai. But the army of Ai defeated the children of Israel. It was due to the disobedience of one man. God wanted all the first fruits of Jericho sacrificed to Him, but one man named Achan held back what belonged to God, and it caused Israel to be defeated. Then God destroyed Achan and his family because of Achan's disbelief and selfishness. Some of you keep holding back the first fruits that God has told you to give, and you keep wondering why you can't win or get ahead.

The only time Israel was defeated by their enemies was when sin was in the camp. There is something about sin that will stop your faith and cause you to be defeated.

Storms come against us all, but when you're walking in God's will, your enemies will be defeated. Yes, you will have battles in your life, but your enemies cannot win. When you are walking in God's will, you can weather every storm that comes against you.

> *What a wonderful thing to know, when your life is right with God no weapon formed against you shall prosper.*

You know the stories about Jonah and Paul. Jonah disobeyed God and the storm almost killed him. Paul loved God and was not in sin. When the storm came against him, he and all with him survived and landed on the island of Malta. As Paul was gathering sticks to put on a fire, a poisonous snake bit his hand. But he just rose up and shook the snake off into the fire and went on with his life. (Acts 27:1–28:10).

What a wonderful thing to know, when your life is right with God no weapon formed against you shall prosper. That alone ought to make someone give up their lover. That alone ought to make someone put down the crack pipe? That alone ought to make you pay your tithes and quit cheating on your taxes.

If you really want to know about the blessings and curses, read Deuteronomy 28. If you walk in obedience to Him, you'll be blessed, your children will be blessed, your dog will be blessed, your chickens will be blessed, and you'll be blessed no matter where you are. You can reverse the curse, if you'll do what's right.

> God doesn't intend for you to lack anything or to be broke. He doesn't intend for you to be sick or living under the curse. It's time to say, "I'm going to reverse this thing in my life."

God doesn't intend for you to lack anything or to be broke. He doesn't intend for you to be sick or living under the curse. It's time to say, "I'm going to reverse this thing in my life."

Every day is a test. "Well, Bishop, I've never had so much trouble in my life. I started serving God with all my heart, and I've never had so much trouble in my life." It's the test. It's all part of what you believe. "Well, Bishop, I don't believe this Bible business, I don't believe anything you're saying today." Honey, some things are true whether you believe it or not. Your beliefs do not alter the truth.

You don't have to go through the same storms year after

year. You can get things turned around in your life in the next few months if you'll make some right choices—and reverse the curse. You need to know that you're blessed or cursed by your own actions. If you'll walk away from ungodly relationships, God promises to bless you in due season. I know you don't want to be alone, and I know you are lonely, but God is going to bless you if you'll do the right thing.

If you'll get serious with God, there is no telling what He will do in the next few months. This is for anyone who is sick and tired of living in the desert. It's for anyone who is sick and tired of living under depression. It's for anyone who is sick and tired of going to jail. It's for anyone who is sick and tired of living under the spirit of failure.

You may be hurting today, but if you'll put the Lord first, it's only a matter of time until He starts turning things around. It's only a matter of time until you walk in victory instead of defeat. That's why you have to forgive people of the things they've done. If you forgive them, God will forgive you. You can't take any chances of walking under the curse anymore, so just forgive them all.

I don't care if you are so broke you can't rub two nickels

together. I'm writing a special delivery letter to you. If you put the Lord first, you can reverse the curse. If you'll put the Lord first, your blessing will come. If you'll put the Lord first, He'll help you find the right kind of husband or wife.

The Lord will help you pay your bills. He'll help you get that job if you put the Him first. He will meet all your needs according to His riches in glory (Philippians 4:19). I know you've messed everything up, and you've made some bad decisions, but you can reverse the curse in Jesus' name.

Job was a man who loved God. Even though he lost his family and his finances, he kept on trusting God and forgiving everybody in his life. The result, God gave him double for his trouble.

The Gospel of Jesus Christ is very clear: No matter how many mistakes you've made, you can

> *The Gospel of Jesus Christ is very clear: No matter how many mistakes you've made, you can repent and watch God move, turn it around, and reverse the curse.*

repent and watch God move, turn it around, and reverse the curse. The Bible says to be subject to God, resist the devil, and he will flee (James 4:7). But before the devil will flee, you have to be submitted to God. You can't do your own thing and say, "Devil, I rebuke you." The devil will laugh as he beats you silly. Obey God and be blessed, disobey God and be cursed.

The Bible says that when the children of Israel removed all the false gods from their lives, the Lord began to bless them. It's time to get rid of anything that's coming between you and Lord. And if you're putting the Lord first, it's only a matter of time until you watch Him reverse the curse. Even though your blessing may be delayed, it cannot be denied if you are walking with the Lord.

> *Paul said to give no place to the devil. That's why the devil is always trying to tempt us with sin so we can bring a curse on our own lives.*

Paul said to come out and be separate (Romans 12:1,2). When we give our lives to the Lord, we're supposed to sever our relationship with worldly things. We are to put on the new self (Ephesians 4:17-24). It's an attitude. That means we stop going places that would cause us to compromise our testimony in the Lord. Maybe you're not going to do anything wrong, but you and I both know there are some places you can no longer go when you sell out to the Lord.

Paul said to give no place to the devil. That's why the devil is always trying to tempt us with sin so we can bring a curse on our own lives. If you're going to walk under the blessing of God, you have to be willing to obey Him no matter what it costs you. Yes, there is a price to pay, but if you are going to sell out to God, you might have to spend some lonely nights. But I'm telling you, it's worth it because God promised to bless you.

Sometimes we have to obey God when we'd rather not obey God. Sometimes we have to say, "God, it hurt me, but I did it for you. God, it cost me, but I did it for you." If you're going to have a breakthrough in your life, sometimes you have to give up those bad relationships you're in. One reason the Lord is allowing you to go through certain things is because He's trying to break your will. That is why you must be certain you are seeking *His* will in order to avoid this cycle of failure.

Because you are diligently obeying God, you must claim the promises that everything will work out in your life. Since you're walking by faith, you don't have to see everything happen today, because you know that in due season you will reap a harvest. Trouble in your life may be a sign you're on the right track. The devil doesn't usually mess with anybody who's going the wrong direction. The terrible resistance you are receiving is probably an indication you have a lot of potential, otherwise why would the devil be fighting you like he is?

When you get on the roller coaster at an amusement

park, they'll tell you, "If you'll pull the bar towards you, don't stand up or turn to the right or the left, you'll make it to the other side." God says, "If you will obey Me and don't turn

> God says, "If you will obey Me and don't turn to the left or to the right, if you'll do what I tell you, you'll make it to the other side" (Joshua 1:7,8).

to the left or to the right, if you'll do what I tell you, you'll make it to the other side" (Joshua 1:7,8). You may be going through hell and high water right now, but you're going to have success in your life. Once you've made up your mind to put God first, you can believe God to reverse the curse.

God said, "I have set before you the blessing and the curse." Your flesh says, "Oh, this doesn't work, I'm going to live it up." But everything you touch fails. There is so much strife in your family that you don't even want to go home. You think that you need some Prozac because of all the depression in your life. But God says, you need to make different choices that will bring you the blessing.

Let me tell you this, when you sell out to the Lord it does not mean you are perfect. It doesn't mean you don't make mistakes or you don't fail. It simply means that when you fail, you don't stay there and wallow in your failure. You need to say, "God, I'm sorry. I need your forgiveness, please turn this thing around." Then, you get up and go on. Your choices have caused you to be where you are right now. But your choices today will take you to the blessing and reverse the curse in your life. Your choices determine whether you have leftovers and God's best.

Now, it won't happen overnight. The messes in our lives didn't happen over night, and the messes aren't going to get fixed overnight either. You're going to feel the blessing, but you may not see the manifestation of the blessing for a while. That is where faith comes in. The just shall walk by faith and not by sight. Trust in the Lord

> The just shall walk by faith and not by sight. Trust in the Lord and watch Him reverse the curse (Proverbs 3:5,6).

and watch Him reverse the curse (Proverbs 3:5,6). Diligently obey God and watch Him command His blessings upon you.

9

DESTINY DECISIONS

Under the new covenant when you give your life to the Lord Jesus Christ, you become an heir of promise. You become the firstborn son of promise whether you are male or female. So when God calls you a son in the new covenant, He's not being sexist. He's not talking just to men, He's talking to men and women as heirs of promise.

He says in this passage, if you are living according to the flesh you must die. In other words, as long as you are living according to the flesh you are out of fellowship with God, and you will not be able to be led by the Spirit of God.

If you love the Lord, you need to know what God's perfect will is for your life. You need to know which school to attend. You need to know which house to buy. You need to know which church God is calling you to attend. If you are single, you need to know which person or persons you should date, as well as those you shouldn't date. If you are living for the Lord, you need to know His perfect will in your life.

No matter who you are, God has a purpose and a destiny just for you. The question is, are you pursuing your destiny and God's perfect will, or are you just floating along through life hoping that everything works out? If you are in His will, you will have success. Notice, I didn't say you wouldn't be tested, but if you are in His will you will make it.

> No matter who you are, God has a purpose and a destiny just for you.

What is your destiny? God calls people into all walks of life. He doesn't just call people to be preachers. He calls people to be schoolteachers, music directors, policemen, and secretaries. Now that you've given your life to the Lord, your vocation is your ministry. I don't care if you are in the construction business or a secretary.

If you're trying to do something you are not called to, you will end up being very unhappy. You can even be unhappy as a pastor if you are not called to do it. You can be unhappy in the choir, if God did not call you there. In fact, the people who will cause the most trouble in the church are people in positions that God did not call them to. If you hate what you are doing right now with your life, it's probably because you are not in your purpose, you are not in your destiny. When you are in God's will, you'll find happiness.

Years ago God was talking to me about walking away from my business to be in ministry. It was on of the hardest decisions I've ever had to make because in my mind I had to walk away from security and all of the things that I worked for. I had to walk away from that in order to be what God had asked me to be. God has now blessed me mightily, but I didn't know then what would

> *...the people who will cause the most trouble in the church are people in positions that God did not call them to.*

happen. For years I received no salary as the pastor of the church.

And for years I made tremendous sacrifices for the ministry, but I had extraordinary joy. I had marvelous peace. Even though the money wasn't there, I had the peace of God in my life. Now, in recent years God has blessed me exceedingly, abundantly beyond all I can possibly ask or think.

You know, when you're making destiny decisions, there's

a lot of pressure on you because you don't want to make any mistakes. Destiny decisions can cause you to walk the floor in the middle of the night.

> You have to step out in faith because you'll never find your destiny until you say, "Lord, not my will, but Thy will be done."

You have to step out in faith because you'll never find your destiny until you say, "Lord, not my will, but Thy will be done." That's why you need to make some tough decisions today. That's why you need to make some choices starting right now. You'll totally miss God's will for your life unless you make right choices, and those right choices begin right now. If you'll chose to do things God's way, you'll be blessed, but if you choose to do things your way, you will end up being cursed.

In spite of the uncertainty, the choices you make today will determine your destiny tomorrow. And that's why you have to seek God with all your heart and get right with Him. You have to get into church. You have to pursue God's will for your life. As I said earlier, you are where you are now because of the choices you've made in the past. You can't blame society for where you are. You can't blame your ex-spouse because of where you are. You can't even blame your parents because of where you are.

If you are going to find your destiny, you have to let go of relationships that you know are not good for you. The truth is you can't waste another ten years making bad choices. You can't wander in the wilderness for another five years. Time is precious. You have to know what He is saying about your destiny and about your life.

> *Are you willing to walk away from the person you are dating in order to be in God's perfect will?*

Are you willing to walk away from the person you are dating in order to be in God's perfect will? Oh, I don't mean he or she is a bad person, but if they're not God's choice for you, you could end up in the biggest mess of your life. That's because marriage will either be heaven on earth, or it will be an earthly hell. If you're going to have a good marriage, you must be equally yoked and have the power of agreement in your lives.

You can't help where you have been, but you can help where you are going. And even if you are not perfect, you've got to know that God has a destiny and a purpose for your life. That's why you have to let go of the past. That's why you have to quit going back to the familiar.

Sometimes we don't want to give up a career because it's like an old shoe. It's comfortable, and you don't want to give it up, but you know you should just throw it away and start over. Sometimes a career is like a relationship; it's comfortable, but it may not be God's best for you.

I don't know about you, but I've made up my mind that I'm not going to waste any more time. I have to find out what God has to say. I can't be doing my thing and then saying, "God, did I do the right thing?" I have to find out what God has to say about it. That's why we all must be led by the Spirit of God, so we can be sure we're making the right decisions in our lives.

> Destiny decisions will cause you to get in the Word like never before. Destiny decisions will cause you to pray like you've never prayed before.

Destiny decisions will cause you to get in the Word like never before. Destiny decisions will cause you to pray like you've never prayed before. Destiny decisions will cause you to seek God like you never have before. And make no mistake, if you are in His perfect will, you are going to be happier than if you are not in His will. Now I'm not talking about God's permissive will; I'm talking about His perfect will. There's a difference between permissive will and perfect will.

You'll do more for God's kingdom if you're in His perfect will than if you're outside His perfect will. But, being in God's perfect will isn't always easy because sometimes it means you're swimming upstream, against the current. It's like trying to drive up a one-way street when all the traffic is flowing against you. When God is leading you, it is not easy. In fact, the truth is, the flesh is against the Spirit and the Spirit is against the flesh. Make no mistake, your flesh will fight the will of God. But if you diligently obey Him, He will command His blessings on you.

> *Anytime you make up your mind to follow the Lord's will, you can bet that opposition will come your way.*

Anytime you make up your mind to follow the Lord's will, you can bet that opposition will come your way. In fact, your spiritual enemy has a plan to deliberately mislead you in some way, and that's why must always go back to the Word. "God, what are you telling me, what are you saying in the Word?" If you are trying to find God's perfect will for your life, you'll never find it outside of His Word.

God and His Word are always in agreement. That's how God talks to you. He doesn't usually speak to you in a loud voice. Instead, He'll lead you by His Spirit. Or you'll be in the Word and nothing is clicking, then all of a sudden, boom!, you gain an insight, sort of like a rocket going off on the inside of you.

If you want to be in God's perfect will, you have to diligently obey the Lord your God. I didn't say God was mad at you, and I didn't say He wouldn't love you. I'm just telling you, you are not going to find His will until you diligently obey the Lord your God and are careful to do all He tells you to do. You have to come into simple obedience. It's not a magic formula, it's just simple obedience. "God, you told me, and I'm doing it." It's simple obedience.

> If you expect God to lead you by His Spirit, you have to get your heart right and you have to do right.

If you expect God to lead you by His Spirit, you have to get your heart right and you have to do right. You have to obey the Word when you don't feel like obeying the Word because the Christian life is about choices. Every single day I am faced with a multitude of choices. Every single day I have got to get my flesh under subjection. Every single day I have to be in the Word, and every single day I have to trust Him. Every day I make choices that will determine my tomorrow.

The Bible says that God and His Word are one. In other words, God's primary way of leading people is by His Word. As you study His word, God is going to reveal His will in your spirit now that you are born again. It all starts in the

Word. We don't tithe because we feel like it. We tithe because God's Word tells us to.

I had a lady inform me that God told her it was okay to marry her unsaved boyfriend because, after they got married, she was going to lead him to the Lord. Whew! Stupid goes clear to the bone. I just stepped on somebody's toes, so I need to clean this up a little bit. The problem we have with that statement is that it contradicts the Word, because God would never tell her to go ahead and marry her unsaved boyfriend because He has already said, "Do not be unequally yoked." He would never contradict Himself. And I will tell you, this lady lived a horrible life for years until they finally got a divorce. Listen, if you marry the wrong person, it can set you back for a long time.

If you go to the wrong church, it can keep you from getting blessed. You know sometimes mama will say, "Go to church with me." And this is the same church your grandma and all of you have been going to forever. But sometimes you have to say, "Mama, leave me alone because I have to follow where God is leading me; I have to go where the Spirit of God is leading me, and I have to get out of this cold, dead church." May I say, if God called you to a warm, friendly church where Jesus Christ is the central focus and where the Word of God is preached and honored, you'd better listen to what He is telling you. You'll probably flourish in that church. However, if you leave a church simply because your feelings have been hurt, you may have a wilderness experience for a long time.

> *If you will be patient in prayer, in a few days things will begin to get clearer.*

One reason why people have such a hard time finding God's will is because they are not in His Word. It's God's Word that will lead you and show you what to do. If you think that God has spoken to you about something, write it down and check it against the Word. Take your time and wait on the Lord. Too often people pray and then try to force things to be the way they want them to be.

If you will be patient in prayer, in a few days things will begin to get clearer. Sometimes finding God's will isn't as hard as you think it is when you take the pressure off and chill. The Word says, "Be still and know that I am God." Sometimes you need to just pray and be still. Sometimes when you are trying to find God's will, all you have to do is ask yourself, "What would the Lord want me to do here?" It's not as hard as you might think it is. When praying, ask yourself, "How would He want me to respond to this situation? What would the Lord want me to do or refrain from doing? What would He want me to do differently?"

Let me say that you cannot be calling the psychic if you expect God to lead you by His Spirit. "But, Bishop, I called the psychic, and she knew all my business." Honey, don't you think the devil knows all your business? He's been watching you, he's been plotting against you and he knows everything about you.

You don't want the devil telling you who to marry or how to invest your money because it's all a lie to trap and steal from you. The Bible says that the devil disguises himself as an angel of light. His plan is to deceive you so he can lead you away from God's will, away from God's plan, away from your destiny. Let me tell you the devil doesn't come to us with two horns and a tail in a little red

> *The Bible says that the devil disguises himself as an angel of light. His plan is to deceive you so he can lead you away from God's will...*

suit. He comes to us disguised as a pretty box. The devil comes to you in tight blue jeans. You see, on the outside everything could look perfectly fine. But, remember, just because you meet someone in church doesn't mean they're the package for you. Maybe it was a set-up by your spiritual enemy in order to steal your destiny?

One of the biggest mistakes we Christians make is

thinking we heard from God when we didn't. We have to be very careful in this area. And when it comes to personal emotions, we have to be very cautious as well; in fact, you cannot trust yourself when it comes to your emotions. And

> *One reason some people miss God's will is because they pray, then get impatient.*

I know we all make mistakes in this area, including me. There have been so many times I just knew I'd heard from God, and I hadn't, I had missed it. All you can do is say, "God, I'm sorry, I thought I was following You."

Sometimes the weirdest people you will ever meet are those that think they are being led by God, and yet it's nothing but their own flesh. "God told me I was going to marry so and so." Well, maybe He did, and maybe He didn't, but you'd better keep quiet and wait. Why? Because if it's God, it will happen. If it's not, just keep your mouth shut. Otherwise you are going to make a fool out of yourself.

One reason some people miss God's will is because they pray, then get impatient. Others pray, but go ahead and do whatever they want to do and end up getting themselves in trouble, and then they try to blame God.

"Oh, Bishop, I'm so confused, I don't know what to do. I prayed and nothing happened. I prayed and God didn't show me what to do." Let me help you right here. Anytime you pray, and you don't know what to do, don't do anything. Stop, and just wait.

My God is not a God of confusion, but a God of peace. If there is any confusion in your situation, pray and wait. Don't try to force it, just wait. Those that wait on the Lord shall renew their strength. Don't you force it. The Bible says to let the peace of Christ rule in your heart. In other words, let peace direct your life. Let peace help you make the decision. Don't do anything until you have a peace that passes all understanding. If there is uneasiness, wait. Don't let impatience cause you to make wrong decisions. Don't let impatience lead you into a mess.

God's way of leading you is by the inward witness. He leads by His Word and also by His Spirit who lives inside of you. He does not lead you by signs. I don't mean that God can't give you a sign, but let me tell you, if you pray for a sign, the devil can also make sure you get one.

Gideon, an Old Testament believer, received guidance through the fleece from a lamb. (See Judges 6.) Gideon said, "What should I do, God?" But Gideon didn't have the Holy Spirit living inside him as do believers who came after Christ's death and Pentecost. Since Gideon didn't have the inner voice inside that comes from the Holy Spirit, he asked for a sign that what he had heard was correct.

So he put out a fleece (a piece of wool from a lamb), and he said, "God, if you're telling me to go up against the Midianites then when I get up in the morning make sure the fleece is all wet with dew and yet the ground around it is dry." When Gideon got up the next morning, the fleece was wet and the ground around it was dry.

He said, "Okay, God, just in case I misunderstood, I'm going to leave this fleece out again, but tomorrow morning make sure the fleece is all dry but the ground around it is wet." And God honored Gideon's request because Gideon could not be led by the inward witness.

But in the new covenant we are not to be led by signs, we are not to be led by experiences around us. We are to be led by the inward witness and simple obedience to the Word of God. "God, what are You saying?" If I don't know what He is telling me, I wait. And until I've got a clear understanding, I pray and stay in His Word until I know what He is telling me to do.

I remember when I first got saved, I was always looking for a sign. I was always looking for a word from the Lord. When I heard about an evangelist coming to town, I would run over there. When I heard about another evangelist, I would run over there, too, because I was looking for a word from the Lord. I thought I was being spiritual as I was looking for a word from God. What I didn't know is I was being carnal because God expects His people to walk by faith and not by sight. God wanted me to quit looking for a word and just go to His Word and get to know Him for myself, to develop a personal walk of faith.

Jesus said, "An evil and adulterous generation seeketh after a sign" (Matthew 12:39). God wants you to quit looking for a sign and just get in the Word and look for Him. Quit running from this

> *God wants you to quit looking for a sign and just get in the Word and look for Him.*

church and to that church looking for a word. Quit looking for somebody to prophesy over you.

Besides that, if a word of prophecy does come to you, it should be nothing but a confirmation of what God has already put on the inside of you.

I've had a lot of people prophesy over me, but I learned a long time ago, if it's God, it's going to come to pass, and if it's not, it won't. If you are demanding a word from the Lord, the devil will make sure you get a word, his word. That's why you have to be determined to walk by faith and not by sight. Quit looking for a word. Be in the Word and look to the Lord.

Since God is Spirit, He leads by His Spirit and not by voices. I hear people say that God spoke out loud to them. I must say I have never had God speak out loud to me, but you have to be careful of hearing voices. If you know of someone who is hearing voices, it could be the enemy trying to confuse them. God does not lead primarily by voices. He can, but primarily He leads by the inward witness. Jesus said, "My sheep know my voice." So, if you know and love the Lord, you'll know His voice on the inside. That inward witness will never contradict His Word.

If you'll obey God's Word and the leading of His Spirit, you'll be blessed financially, you'll be blessed emotionally, you'll be blessed spiritually, and you'll have contentment in your life. If you want to know about God's leading, simply know He always uses your natural interests to lead you. For example, my wife is a graphic artist. She was a graphic artist in the world, and now He uses her as a graphic artist today. He uses your natural talent.

The truth of the matter is, if I seek Him and obey Him and make Godly decisions every day, it's only a matter of time until my dreams are realized, and I fulfill the destiny and purpose that God has for my life.

You are a product of all the choices you make. I've given you a lot of information to help you make right decisions, but destiny decisions require tough choices. It shall come to pass if you diligently obey the Lord thy God and perform all that He directs you to do, He will command His blessings on you.

No More Leftovers

10

THE GREAT PRETENDER

We humans are great pretenders. We pretend to be something we are not. We pretend to be better singers than we are. We pretend to be better preachers than we are. We pretend to have it all together. We pretend to be something we're not because we have an image to uphold. But it's nothing more than the pride of life.

We act one way in church, and we act a whole different way when we get home. We put on a holy face when we attend church and cuss our spouses and children when we get in the parking lot. Most of us are so prideful we can't even admit that we have pride. I'm talking about the fact that we never say, "I'm sorry." "Why would I say I'm sorry, I didn't do anything wrong." I'm talking about the fact that everyone else is wrong but us. Isn't it amazing that every relationship breaks up the same way, and it's always everyone else's fault.

You go to every church in town and every one of them has a problem except for you. The reason you have to blame everyone else for your failures is because the pride of life will not let you take the responsibility. You see, pride doesn't admit failure, because failure makes you look weak, but God said, "If you will humble yourself under the mighty hand of God, humble yourself under authority, then in due season, I will raise you up." You need to know that if you do not humble yourself, God cannot help you. If you don't humble yourself, God has His ways of dealing with you.

The Titanic was supposed to be a ship that was unsinkable. They said that even God couldn't sink the ship. Their arrogance and pride caused fifteen hundred and twenty two people to go to a watery grave. I'm telling you, arrogance and pride will bring you down.

The Bible says that because of Paul's pride, God allowed a thorn in his flesh to keep him from exalting himself. Now I don't know what his thorn in the flesh was. But whatever it was, God allowed trouble in his life. God knew Paul came out of a religious background, was prone to pride, and had a tendency toward arrogance. So He continually allowed Paul to go through trials to keep him from exalting himself because He knew the inclination toward pride was there.

When God is working in your life, He'll allow some things to come against you in order to break you. Maybe the reason you keep going through the same problems year after year after year has something to do with your pride. Maybe the reason you always live under a spirit of failure is because you cannot take advice and will not listen to other people. Maybe the reason you can't get blessed is because you won't obey the Word?

> *When God is working in your life, He'll allow some things to come against you in order to break you.*

I know you think you are all of that, but in one minute you can lose your beauty or your good looks. In a flash, a car wreck can take it all away. In one instant, trouble can humble you like nothing else can. In one moment a jail term will bring you to your knees. If you want God to use your life for His glory, there's only one thing to do and that's humble yourself. You have to lower yourself before God can raise you up. God can't bless anybody that's high and mighty and thinks they are all of that.

It's amazing how you can get people to sing in the choir,

but you can't get people to work in the church parking lot. If people can't be seen, they don't want to do the job. I'm talking about the pride of life where you have to let everyone see you drive your new car. I'm talking about a special need you have to prove to everyone in your past that you made it.

If you humble yourself before God, He'll lift you up. If you'll admit your failures, He'll raise you higher.

If you humble yourself before God, He'll lift you up. If you'll admit your failures, He'll raise you higher. If you'll go to God, He'll lift you when you can't lift yourself. The Bible tells us to clothe ourselves in an attitude of humility. We are to clothe ourselves in patience and gentleness. Through faith and patience we shall obtain the promises of God.

I remember some years ago the Lord dealt with me about my pushiness and aggressiveness. God said, "If you really have faith, you'd be praying and waiting on Me instead of trying to make it happen yourself." Pride says, "Okay, God, I'm not waiting any longer. I've been waiting for my mate long enough, and I'm going to go find one." Humility says, "Lord, I'm going to put it in Your hands. I'm going to wait on You. I'm going to trust in You, because I'm in submission to You." Pride is about me, me, me. Pride is about getting my needs met, but humility is about meeting the needs of others.

A humble person is a servant. Anytime people humble themselves, God will use them for His glory. Anytime someone gives God all the credit for the things that He has done in their lives, He will raise them up. Anytime someone says, "Lord, I am weak, You are

> *A humble person is a servant. Anytime people humble themselves, God will use them for His glory.*

strong," then God will move in to help and strengthen them. Anytime someone says, "God, I'm a hypocrite, I need Your help," then God will move in to help them and show them a better way. I don't know about you, but I'm not too proud to say, "Lord, I need Your help. I'm nothing without You, I am weak, and You are strong. Lord, forgive me of my arrogance, forgive me of my pride, forgive me for being a great pretender."

I'm trying to tell you that we should quit trying to be something we aren't. Quit trying to impress people. Be yourself and know that God broke the mold when He made you. You are unique. There's nobody else like you, and you don't have to try to be like anyone else. God has a special plan for your life, and nobody can fulfill that plan but you.

Now God said He's opposed to the proud but gives grace to the humble (James 4:6). I don't know about you, but I could use a little more grace. So what can I do to humble myself? Who can I forgive? Can I be honest and admit my failures? Can I be honest and admit that I am arrogant and prideful?

One time I told the Lord how ambitious I was, and He answered, "You're not ambitious, you're full of pride. You want everyone to think you're ambitious, but the truth is pride is driving you." The Bible says, "Confess your faults to one another so that you may be healed" (James 5:16). In other words, if you can't confess your pride and arrogance, you can't even get healed. You are having everyone in town lay hands on you because you're sick, but the reason you can't get healed is because of your pride.

> *One time I told the Lord how ambitious I was, and He answered, 'You're not ambitious, you're full of pride.*

When I confess areas of pride in my life, God strengthens me. God showed me years ago to confess my faults to my congregation. The end result, the more I confess my faults to my church, the stronger I get. When you humble yourself to say, "You know, I really am an arrogant so-and-so, but God is working on me, pray for me," God can use that. The reason that God can't help some people is because they won't deal with their pride. There are some prayers God cannot answer until you humble yourself. He can't even bring you out of the wilderness until you humble yourself.

You will continue to live under a spirit of failure until you humble yourself and recognize who you are and who you are not. The reason you have such a hard time forgiving others is the pride of life. Your mind says, "I can't believe they did that to me, I can't believe they said that about me. After all I've done for them." I don't forgive you because I want to; I forgive you because if I don't, God isn't going to forgive me. If I don't humble myself to forgive you, God will have to humble me.

> *You will continue to live under a spirit of failure until you humble yourself and recognize who you are and who you are not.*

Pride will keep you from saying you're sorry. Sometimes you need to say you're sorry even when you're not, just to humble yourself. Pride will cause you to avoid somebody for years.

Pride will cause you to run away from the church God called you to because you got hurt there. Your pride was offended and you left mad.

Pride will keep you from praising God the way you

should. Pride will keep you from raising your hands. Pride will keep you from shouting unto God with the voice of triumph. Pride will keep you off your knees. Pride will never let you bow before anyone or anything.

Pride is the pastor who says I will build the biggest church in town. Pride is a church leader who says we're the only ones going to heaven. Pride is the person who never answers an altar call. Pride is the person who always interrupts because they've got more to say than you.

> Pride is the person who thinks he or she is better than someone else.

Pride is the religious person who says he's glad he's not as bad as others. Pride is the person who can't be told what to do. Pride is the person who cannot humble themselves under authority because they've got all the answers, and they know more than the person to whom they should submit.

Pride is the person who thinks he or she is better than someone else. Pride is the person who's full of prejudice and racism. Pride is the person who thinks this message is not for him or her, but for someone else.

The reason you keep gossiping about that person at work is because your pride has been hurt. The reason you keep talking about the things they did to you, and you won't let it go, is because your pride has been wounded. You see there is something about pride that causes us to backbite other people. The spirit behind pride is judgmental, and it can lead you to talk about others to bring them down. And in some perverse way, doing so makes you feel stronger and

> *If you don't humble yourself, you will have nothing but leftovers all of your life.*

better. But you need to be careful because the Word says by the standard you use to judge others is the standard that God will use to judge you (Matthew 7:2).

God says, "I know all about you, and you've got no reason to be arrogant." God says, "I know about you behind closed doors." He says, "I know where you were last Thursday, and I know what you were doing. You're acting holy now, but I know whom you were with and what you were doing."

If you don't humble yourself, you will have nothing but leftovers all of your life. If you don't humble yourself, you'll live under the spirit of failure all of your life. If you don't humble yourself, you will never see a healing miracle in your life; you'll never see a restoration miracle in your life. But the moment you humble yourself and pray, God will move in to help you. The moment you say, "God, I can't do it without you," He begins the process of bringing you out.

We all need to constantly be looking at ourselves and repenting. About the time I think I've got it going on, that ugly thing of pride sticks up his head. Every once in a while I catch myself and pray, "God, forgive me of that pride, forgive me of that arrogance in my life." Every once in a while we have to say, "Lord, I know I'm a great pretender, but I ask you to forgive me. I see that pride in my life, and I ask you to wash me clean. I'm ready for all your blessings. So I repent of my pride and ask you to turn everything around."

> *We all need to constantly be looking at ourselves and repenting. About the time I think I've got it going on, that ugly thing of pride sticks up his head.*

11

Truth or Consequences

The Bible tells us there are seven things that are an abomination to God. One of those things is a lying tongue. God's Word even says that all liars will burn in the second death. It also tells us that lying is a part of our sin nature. Infants don't have to be taught to lie. The nature of the flesh is to lie in order to get what we want or to escape punishment. I don't care how great a parent you are, or how often you bring your children to church, your children will learn to lie. Even as toddlers, it's only a matter of time until they say, "Mommy, I didn't do it," and you know they're lying to you.

Before we gave our hearts to the Lord, we would lie to get what we wanted. We would lie to better our positions at work. We would lie to get more money. We would even lie to get sex. Jesus said that the devil is a liar and the father of all lies (John 8:44). So, anytime we lie, we are siding with the enemy. That's why we have to make up our minds to tell the truth. We need to decide before hand that we not are going to lie, because in sticky situations our pride enters in, and we may be strongly tempted to lie to make ourselves look better. We always try to position ourselves in such a way that we seem to be better than we are.

> *Paul told us to put away all lying. Now that we love the Lord, our nature should be to always tell the truth, the whole truth, and nothing but the truth.*

Paul told us to put away all lying. Now that we love the Lord, our nature should be to always tell the truth, the whole truth, and nothing but the truth. When we catch ourselves telling a lie we need to stop, confess it, and then turn from it. The Bible plainly tells us that God hates lying. He hates lying because it's opposite His pure, moral character. Anytime we are not honest, we are lining ourselves up with Satan, and setting ourselves up for failure. Until you learn to do what is right and tell the truth, you will never overcome the spirit of failure that has been on your family for generations. Until you tell the truth, you will always have leftovers and hand-me-downs in your life.

The ninth commandment in the Bible says, "Thou shalt not bear false witness." In other words, you shall not lie because of the enormous damage and destruction it brings. Jesus said, "I am the Way, the Truth, and the Life." Anytime we are true disciples of Jesus Christ, His Spirit in us will cause us to tell the truth.

Let me say this too, if you are a controller and a manipulator, then you are probably a liar as well. Manipulators will exaggerate the truth to get what they want. They will tell a partial truth, which is, in actuality, a whole lie.

> *...if you are a controller and a manipulator, then you are probably a liar as well. Manipulators will exaggerate the truth to get what they want.*

Some years ago the Lord dealt with me about not exaggerating when I preach. The Lord spoke to my heart and told me He did not need my help stretching the truth in order to make my point. Now that we love the Lord, God wants us to grow and work on our character. I know you're thinking about somebody right now who's a liar, but let me tell you, the moment you point one finger to judge someone else, you have three pointing right back at you.

God expects us, as believers, to walk with integrity.

People should know they can trust you. They should know that your word counts for something. They should know that when you give your word, it's as good as gold. As Christians, there is always a continual fight inside us. The old man fights the new man. The flesh fights the spirit. Good fights evil. Light fights darkness.

> *God wants us to be honest, and He wants us to be so honest that we tell the truth even if it costs us our reputation, even if it costs us money.*

God wants us to be honest, and He wants us to be so honest that we tell the truth even if it costs us our reputation, even if it costs us money. You see, we're talking about character and integrity issues. Character is more important than your money. Now the real point is this, can God trust you? God will only give you as much as He can trust you with. If you don't have anything, and you haven't had anything for a long time, that might be an indication that God can't trust you with any more than what you already have.

You'll never be what God wants you to be as long as you tell little white lies. As long as you lie to protect your reputation, God can't trust you. I'll even go so far as to say, if you lie to protect somebody else, God can't trust you. God doesn't want us living a lie; He wants us to be honest and live the truth. His Word is truth.

God wants us to live in truth and not in falsehoods. He doesn't want us living one way on Sunday and another way on Monday. He doesn't want us to be a public success and a private failure. You look like you've got it all together when you come to church, but after you leave, you are falling apart and you're cussing your spouse out in the car.

> *Some of you are wrestling with character issues that you should have settled a long time ago.*

Some of you are wrestling with character issues that you should have settled a long time ago. Some of you have refused to do what is right, and now God is bringing you a word of warning in this book. One of the key reasons we lie is our stupid pride. You'll tell a lie because you don't want somebody to think poorly of you because you don't know the answer, you don't have enough money, or you really didn't graduate.

So let me ask you, what kind of reputation do you have? Because, you see, your reputation always precedes you. Do people trust you or do they not trust you? Do they trust you to hold the money? Do they trust you to carry the keys? Do they believe you when you tell them something or do they question what you say? Do they have confidence in you or not? What do you do when the bill collectors call on the phone? Do you have your children answer and lie for you? "Hello, Daddy says he's not here. Mommy says she's not here either." What do you do when somebody gives you too much change? Do you think God blessed you? I'm talking about character and integrity issues for a believer. If you diligently obey God, He will command His blessings on you.

> *What do you do when somebody gives you too much change? Do you think God blessed you? I'm talking about character and integrity issues for a believer.*

You see, when you say you're going to do something, do you do it? Do you pay your bills on time? Do you know that Christians have a horrible reputation for not paying their bills on time? I don't mean to offend anyone, but if you are consistently late in paying your bills, then you are not a person of integrity, and you are not a person of your word. It is more than bad credit, it's about who you are. It's about your character and what you are made of.

Webster's dictionary says that a person of integrity is someone you can trust. Can I trust you to be on time? If you tell me you're going to be there at 6:30, do you show up at 7:00? Can I trust you not to steal time? Can I trust you to cover my back? The word *Christian* means "Little Christ." If you call yourself a Christian, then you ought to be a "Little Christ." If you are consistently late wherever you go, may I suggest that you need to make some changes in your life. If you don't do what you say, then God is talking to you about your character and what you are made of.

Unfortunately, most Americans have lost their sense of integrity. Companies advertise inferior products and praise their qualities. Yet everybody suspects they are lying and just trying to boost company sales. Salesmen exaggerate the truth in order to move more products and make more money. No matter who we are, we all seem to justify our lying in some way. But make no mistake, lying is of the devil, and God hates it. People steal on their jobs because they feel they're not paid enough. They steal time because they feel like they're not appreciated. God calls it lying.

When people turn in false insurance claims, it's a lie, it's dishonest, and God hates it. Let me say it another way, if you do this kind of thing, you are a liar, and God cannot help you. You will always live under a curse, you will always

> *If you are consistently late wherever you go, may I suggest that you need to make some changes in your life.*

live under the spirit of failure until you make up your mind to obey God, do what's right, and trust in Him. Make no mistake, no matter who you are, your sin will surely find you out.

When God is working in your life, He won't let you get away with sin. You think, because He loves you, He's going to let you get away with it. It's because He loves you that He won't let you get away with it. The problem is, if you get away with something for awhile, you'll think it's okay, and your conscience will be dulled. But God will expose you, and that's why He says, "Judge yourself so I won't have to."

> When God is working in your life, He won't let you get away with sin. You think, because He loves you, He's going to let you get away with it.

If you lie or cheat to get something, you will eventually lose it. Whatever you lie to get, you will lose. Whatever you cheat to get, you will lose. That's because God is watching, and what man sows that shall he also reap (Galatians 6:7). You cannot outrun the laws of His Word. The Bible says, "A false witness shall not go unpunished, and he that speaketh lies shall perish" (Proverbs 19:5). We're talking about truth or consequences.

Anytime you stretch the truth to make a sale, you are

lying. Anytime you are not honest in a relationship, you are living a lie. Character is what you are made of. An adulterer is nothing more than a lie and a cheat. It's about character. You may think, "My spouse doesn't understand me, therefore, it's okay to do this," but it's about your faulty character.

> Lying doesn't pay off in the long run because God is watching everything. Whatever you give out is what you get back. I'm talking about truth or consequences.

Lying doesn't pay off in the long run because God is watching everything. Whatever you give out is what you get back. I'm talking about truth or consequences. Tell the truth or you're going to have consequences to pay. If you don't tell the truth, you are going to have to pay the price. You may get away with it today, but I'm telling you, you will not get away with it forever. I'm talking about asking God to change your heart.

The Lord is saying if you trust in Him you'll be blessed, but if you harden your heart, you'll have lots of trouble. When you have lied enough, your heart becomes hardened. It's amazing when people lie constantly, eventually they start believing their own lies. They are convinced they told the truth and now they believe their own lies. The problem is they told a lie, and now they need to tell another lie to cover up the lie and keep from getting caught in that lie.

If you belong to the Lord, He'll put you on the potter's wheel, and He'll begin to spin that wheel. Sometimes you may think your life is spinning out of control, but God says, " I've got to spin you, I've got to reform you. Sometimes I might even have to crush or dig something out of you that doesn't belong inside you." God says, "I love you enough to let you go to jail, so I can stop you now before your behavior gets further out of control."

> Psalm 15 says, "Whom may live in God's presence? Only those who walk with integrity and do not lie."

Psalm 15 says, "Whom may live in God's presence? Only those who walk with integrity and do not lie." In other words, you will never truly dwell in the presence of the Lord until you work on your integrity and stop your lying. I know you've been Slick Sally or Sammy for a long time, but God wants to change your name, He wants to change your character, He wants to change the direction of your life, and He wants to make you a person of integrity.

I know people who are so talented it would blow your mind, but they don't have integrity. I know people who love the Lord, but they have such faulty character that God can't really use them to any extent. I know folk who have been saved for years, but when you talk to them you don't know whether they are telling you the truth or whether they are lying. Yes, the Bible says that, "the gifts and callings of God are without repentance" (Romans 11:29). The gifts are irrevocable that God hands out, but let me tell you your gift will make room for you. It can even take you to the top, but if you don't have integrity, you will come down like a house of cards.

God is so awesome when you use your faith. He'll open doors for your ministry. He'll do things for you that will blow your mind, but you'll have to work on your character. Your talent can take you places, but it's your character that will keep you there, or cause you to fail. You can have all the right moves, you can wear all the right clothes, and you can have all the contacts in the mayor's office, but

> *God is so awesome when you use your faith. He'll open doors for your ministry. He'll do things for you that will blow your mind, but you'll have to work on your character.*

if you don't work on your character, you will always live under a spirit of failure. You'll live under a curse.

There's somebody right now reading this book that has a secret life. I'm telling you, that secret life will destroy you. I'm telling you that God cannot bless you when you are living a lie. You keep waiting for God to open the doors to your ministry or to your business, but God's waiting for you to work on your character. You keep waiting for God to help you get a house, but He's waiting for you to clean up your credit so you can get a house. If you've been saved for a while and still haven't cleaned up your credit, God is trying to get your attention right now.

> You keep waiting for God to bring you a platform, but He's waiting for you to work on your integrity.

You keep waiting for God to bring you a platform, but He's waiting for you to work on your integrity. You keep waiting for God to give you a greater anointing, and He keeps talking to you about your integrity. He keeps talking to you about doing what's right. Doing what's right is not flirting with the married person at the office. You have to think more of yourself than that anyway. You can't live for leftovers. God cares more about your integrity than He does your gifts. He cares more about your moral qualities than He does about you getting a new car.

God wants to know what do you do when nobody's looking? He wants to know what you do when you're out of town, and nobody knows your name. I'm talking about who you really are. I'm talking about the character and integrity in which you walk. You see, God cares more about your character than He does the way you sing. He cares more about your character than the way you play your musical instrument. He cares more about your character than He does the way you preach.

You may become a deacon, but if you don't have good character you can't be trusted. Your sins will find you out. You may have more degrees than a thermometer, but if you're a liar, you can't be trusted. You don't measure a man's integrity by how he acts in church on Sunday. You don't measure his integrity by how loud he can shout or how good he can dance in church. You measure his integrity by his honesty and how he conducts his life and whether he does what's right or not.

Character is developed when your flesh tells you to do one thing, but you obey God and do what He says instead. Character is developed when you have a good excuse not to show up, but you're faithful, press through all the trouble and you show up anyway. Character is developed when everything and everyone around you tells you, "It's okay; everybody's doing it." But you're determined to do what's right, you're determined to do it God's way, because you're determined to get out from underneath that spirit of failure that's been doggin' you all your life.

If you lie and it doesn't bother you, then your heart has become hardened to the Spirit of God, and He is asking you to examine yourself and take the mask off. His Word says,

> The Bible says, "Lying lips are an abomination to the Lord" (Proverbs 12:22). No wonder some folks live under the spirit of failure.

"Sanctify yourself today and tomorrow you will see wonders in your midst" (Joshua 3:5). You keep wondering why nothing works out in your life. It's because you're cheating and you're lying, and God cannot bless you. The Bible says, "Lying lips are an abomination to the Lord" (Proverbs 12:22).

No wonder some folks live under the spirit of failure. No wonder some folk are always in trouble. No wonder it seems like nothing works out in their lives. Let me tell you something about liars. If you consistently lie, you will probably be a person that's weak in faith. If you lie, you'll have a hard time believing God. If you're a liar, you won't even believe that God has told you the truth.

The reason God is allowing all this trouble in your life right now is because He is wrestling with you concerning your character and integrity. He's wrestling with you concerning the direction of your life.

Make no mistake, because He loves you, He will let you

go into the fiery trial (1 Peter 4:12). You may be binding the devil, but the devil doesn't have a thing to do with this. This has to do with God trying to change you. God is trying to burn some things out of you. He is trying to rattle your cage and get your attention. Because He loves you, God will do everything possible to burn that deceit out of you before it's too late.

When you're a baby, you just do what you want to, but when you grow up you begin to say, "Wait a minute. I have to be responsible for my own actions." When you grow up in Christ, you'll stop and say, "Wait a minute, I just lied to you.

> *When you're a baby, you just do what you want to, but when you grow up you begin to say, "Wait a minute. I have to be responsible for my own actions."*

Let me correct this situation." When you get to that point, it won't take long, and you'll overcome your lying.

Holiness is not so much about the way you dress. It's not about how long your dress is. It's not whether you scrub all the makeup off your face and put your hair back in a bun and take all of your jewelry off. That's not holiness. Even though you have to commend anyone who would do anything they could to have more holiness in their lives, true holiness has to do with the condition of your heart. Holiness has to do with obeying God, rather than doing what you want to do. It's about putting God first and getting your heart right.

How are people going to be attracted to the Jesus you preach unless you're a man or woman of integrity? What if you're preaching Jesus, and they catch you in a lie. It's time to take off the mask. It's time to go before God in honesty. It's time to stand in His presence and say, "Lord, I'm a liar, I need your help, I have faulty character, and I want you to change me."

You don't have to be perfect to go to heaven, but to be effective and used of God, you must repent of your lying and cheating and become honest and trustworthy. You have to withstand the downward pull of the enemy and put on God's nature in your life. If you're going to fulfill your destiny, you have to be honest and go on to a higher level than where you are. To be a true servant of the Lord, you have to be truthful. If you want to overcome the spirit of failure from your past, you have to make up your mind to do what is right and tell the truth. If you want to have God's best in your life, you have to be willing to be obedient.

12

I Am Not The Judge

The Bible warns us not to be judgmental. That warning is necessary because judging is a very natural product of our fallen human nature. Because God knows how difficult it is for us to refrain from judging, He warns us how destructive judging can be not only to those judged, but also to those doing the judging. In fact, the Bible tells us that no matter who we are, we have no right to judge others. We have no right to condemn others for the things they've done wrong or even the mistakes they have made.

The principle in the Word of God is this, the same balance of harshness and mercy you use in judging others will be used to judge you for what you have done. Here again is the idea of sowing and reaping, the standard of measure that you give out is the same standard of measure that comes back.

The Word of God is very clear, if you forgive people a little bit for what they've done, then you will receive a little bit of forgiveness for what you have done. And God says that even though you may feel you are qualified to judge others for what they have done, you are neither the judge nor the jury over them. God says that you are not qualified to sit in judgment.

> You are not qualified to judge others because God says, "I know all about you.

You are not qualified to judge others because God says, "I know all about you. I know where you were a week ago Tuesday night, I know what you did, and who you did it with. Your halo may be spinning today, but I know all about you, and you are not qualified to judge anybody else for the way they have lived their life."

There is a principle in the kingdom of God that says; "Whatever you give out is what you get back. Whatever you sow, that you shall also reap. Judge not, lest you be judged yourself." The point is this, if you have any brains you will pray for folk instead of talking about them behind their back and you judge them.

The Christian author, C. S. Lewis, said the greatest sin in the body of Christ is the sin of judging other Christians. The church is the only army that shoots its wounded. We are the only army that kicks the fallen when they are down.

Any time you judge others, you are telling God to get off His throne, move aside, and let you take over. But you see, God won't let you get away with it because He knows too much about you.

People with an abusive past, tend to be judgmental murmurers and backbiters who end up living in the wilderness, lacking so much in their lives. But you don't have to stay in the wilderness. If you'll begin to make some changes today, God will help you out of your mess. If you will quit judging others, God will help you in supernatural ways.

> *People with an abusive past, tend to be judgmental murmurers and backbiters who end up living in the wilderness...*

The children of Israel lived under a spirit of failure while they were in the wilderness because of all of their murmuring and negative talking. There is something inside us all that inclines us to be self-righteous and judgmental. We tend to be like the publican in the Bible who says, "Oh, I'm glad I'm not as bad as they are" (Luke 18:9-14).

No matter who you are, you can never out run the laws of God. If you are judgmental, you will never have the favor of God in your life because you will always reap what you give out. If you want to get things turned around in your life, you have to learn to pray for people, love people, and quit judging them. If you will obey God's Word, He will help you.

> *If you are judgmental, you will never have the favor of God in your life because you will always reap what you give out.*

A strange thing about human beings is we can never see ourselves quite the way others see us. In life we are, in effect, sitting on top of our baggage, and though we see everyone else's baggage clearly, we can't seem to have a clear picture of our own. So we become judgmental and are blinded by our own pride.

God's Word tells us, when we judge others, we are hypocrites. You see, none of us are perfect, and we've all had a lot of failures, though we try to keep those things hidden from others. God says, "I know what you've been doing, so just keep your nose out of other people's business." Judgmental people always live under a spirit of failure. If you know someone who is judgmental, watch them and see what they get back for their judgmental behavior.

You will never be the success that God wants you to be as long as you are critical and judgmental. Judgment keeps coming back to people who are judgmental of others. Now that you belong to the Lord, He expects you to change. You may be in the wilderness and you may have had an abusive past, but He expects you to change. He expects you to pick up the cross and follow Him. He expects you to grow up in Christ and put down your judgmental attitudes.

> *You will never be the success that God wants you to be as long as you are critical and judgmental. Judgment keeps coming back to people who are judgmental of others.*

If you want to get out of the wilderness, you have to make some changes in your life. And if you want to overcome the spirit of failure, you have to love your neighbor as yourself. You would not judge yourself so harshly, so why would you judge your neighbor in the same way?

There's no love in judgmental attitudes. There's no love in being critical. There's no love in being a backbiter. So when you are judgmental, God brings it back on you. That's why some folk can't get healed. There are some prayers God will not answer until you quit judging other people. I believe the root of all judgmental attitudes is nothing more than pride. We think we are better than someone else, and so we talk about them. And when we talk about others, it's our way of trying to bringing them down and raising ourselves up.

There is something about our pride that makes us think that we don't have the problems they have. Judge not. Until you have walked in someone else's shoes, you don't know what you would do. Until the bottom falls out of your life, you don't know what you would do. It's only when the real pressure comes that you find out what you're really made of.

> *There is something about our pride that makes us think that we don't have the problems they have.*

I'm not trying to make excuses for anybody, so don't misunderstand what I've just said. But I am trying to say, people will reap what they sow, so why not pray for people instead of judging them, because the wages of sin is death (Romans 6:23). If anyone breaks God's laws, God's laws are going to break them. But we need to love each other and have compassion for one another, rather than judging or condemning them.

People are in prison today because of bad choices. They made stupid mistakes, but until you walk in their shoes, you don't know what you would have done. Let me tell you, nobody has a dream of growing up and being a convict. You don't have to judge people; the Word of God will judge them. You don't have to be God's policeman; God can take care of His business. You don't have to judge preachers either, because if they are doing something wrong, God is plenty big enough to bring them down if He wants to. "Judge not, lest you bring judgment back on yourself" (Matthew 7:1). Besides, isn't the church supposed to be a place of love and a place of acceptance? Isn't it supposed to be a place where people who have failed can be encouraged?

> *You don't have to judge people; the Word of God will judge them. You don't have to be God's policeman; God can take care of His business.*

There seems to be a tremendous lack of love in churches today and God hates it. He wants us to be full of grace and mercy, because that is the nature of God. You see, the danger of opening up your arms to sinners is people accuse you of going easy on sin. But I'd rather be accused of going easy on sin and loving folk than I would be of judging them and hurting them.

There's a sign in front of our church that says "Sinners Welcome Here." Now we've had some church folk call us and say, "I can't believe you've got that sign out front. I told you that Bishop Leonard goes easy on sin." We are not condoning your sin. We are saying "Come on in, in spite of your sin and let God clean you up."

Sometimes we can be saved for a long time and forget where we came from. Sometimes we forget the pigpen that God brought us out of. Sometimes you need to remind yourself how far God has brought you, and where you were before Christ saved you.

> Sometimes we can be saved for a long time and forget where we came from. Sometimes we forget the pigpen that God brought us out of.

Religion sees people in their sin and condemns them, but Jesus saw people in their sin and He loved them. He didn't come to judge the world, but to save it (John 3:17). If Jesus didn't come to judge, who do you think you are? If we'd be more concerned about loving sinners rather than judging them, I believe we would see a whole lot more people giving their lives to the Lord than we do.

It's not my job to judge the adulterer, but it is my job to preach the truth in love. It's not my job to judge those who have had an abortion, but it is my job to preach the truth in love. We need to tell everyone that no matter what they've done, God is not mad. Religion may be mad at them, but

God is not mad. When people do things that are wrong, they are going to reap what they sow anyway.

You can get out of the wilderness and you can get out from underneath that spirit of failure, if you begin to judge yourself and stop judging others. Quit pointing your fingers at others, and start pointing at yourself. Quit making excuses for your judgmental attitude and start

> *You can get out of the wilderness and you can get out from underneath that spirit of failure, if you begin to judge yourself and stop judging others.*

judging yourself. Quit condemning others, and God will quit condemning you. "Listen, Bishop, you'll never see me doing what they are doing." Let me tell you, if you're not careful, you may end up worse than they are by bringing judgment back on yourself. Never say never. Just say, "By the grace of God He has kept me from that."

You know the story about the woman that was caught in the act of adultery? Religious folk brought the woman to Jesus to kill her, but Jesus chose to love her instead. You'd be surprised how many religious folk want to use the Word of God to kill you rather than restore you.

It was Paul who said, when a man is caught in sin, do everything you can to restore him in a spirit of gentleness (Gal. 6:1). You see, it's an attitude. It's making up your mind to love people instead of judging people. Under the law, the adulterous woman had to die. She was guilty of her sin, but Jesus came to give her grace, and to restore her in a spirit of love, and a spirit of gentleness. The religious folk could have loved her, but they chose to condemn her. If your religion doesn't love people, what good is your religion?

While the woman and her accusers stood there, Jesus stooped down and began to write in the dirt. We don't know exactly what He wrote, but I think He began to write the sins of the accusers. I may be wrong, but we do know that when Jesus began to write, the religious folk got up and left. I'm telling you that if God put your sins up on a television screen, I don't care how holy you look today, you would have to hold up one finger and tip out of the room. You would have to say, "Excuse me, but I have got to slip out of this room."

Jesus said, "Let him who is without sin cast the first stone" (John 8:7).

You can always spot religious folk because they don't have a clue how to love others. They know what the Word says, but they will try to kill you with their fifty-pound Bible. You know that Jesus didn't care much for religious folk either. He hated their legalism, their judgmental attitude, and He hated the fact that they were as mean as a junkyard dog.

As staff members in the church, we are held to a higher

degree of accountability. It's not because we think we are better than you. We already know that as staff members we are not. But as staff members, we have to be examples to people around us. That doesn't mean if a staff member fails, we kill him or her. It doesn't mean that we kick them out. But we will have to confront sin, and we will have to hold both staff members and regular church members accountable, no matter who they may be.

But when we do fail as staff members and leaders in the church, be careful of the way you judge us and others. By the standard of measure you give out, that same standard is going to come back to you. It's not for anyone to judge, and that's why we should never judge who is saved and who isn't. You see, a baby Christian may not look saved, but be on his or her way to be doing something great for God. So let's let God do the judging.

> *...a baby Christian may not look saved, but be on his or her way to be doing something great for God. So let's let God do the judging.*

Peter said, be fervent in your love for one another, because love covers a multitude of sins (1 Peter 4:8). What do you do when you hear rumors about others? Do you jump to conclusions or do you pray? There is something inside every one of us that immediately wants to jump to conclusions when we hear a piece of juicy negative gossip.

Even if your parents did a poor job raising you, don't judge them. Just know they did the best they could, and all they did was act like their parents did when raising them.

When I sit in the jury box, and I hold things against my parents, all I do is condemn myself. In fact, be careful of judging them, lest you grow up to be just like them. Not only are we to forgive, but if we don't let go of the past, we will end up being exactly like our parents.

> *You'll never have the blessings of God that He wants you to have, as long as you are judgmental.*

Those of you who have been married previously understand that as badly as your ex treated you or as unfair as everything was, God says, "Let it go. Release them and don't judge them." I have learned from personal experience that whatever you bind or hold against others, God holds against you. At least you have an opportunity to get that mess behind you. You see, if you don't let it go, you'll end up marrying someone else that was just like the one that you just divorced.

You'll never have the blessings of God that He wants you to have, as long as you are judgmental. "If I will diligently obey the Lord my God and be careful to do all that He has said, He will command me to be blessed" (Deuteronomy 28:1, 8). That includes judgmental attitudes. I don't know about you, but I need all the blessings I can get. I can't take any chances of *not* having His blessings. Even though I may not agree with your life, I can't take any chances of my judgment coming back on me.

Paul said there's only one person you have a right to judge, and that's yourself. In fact, he said if you judge yourself, God wouldn't have to (1 Corinthians 11:31). You can get your life turned around if you'll make up your mind and say, "God, I'm going to repent of this thing, and I'm going to trust in you."

No More Leftovers

13

I Will Not Be A Failure Forever

The Bible says that when you are born again you will love God and keep His commandments. You know you're on your way to heaven when you want to do God's will even though your flesh is fighting you on it. Being born again doesn't mean you've never failed God, it just means that your heart has been changed, and you want to do right. You may not always do what is right, but you want to do what is right.

If you can sin and it doesn't bother you, there is something wrong in your relationship with the Lord. The Bible says that God's commandments are not burdensome. In other words, because He has changed our hearts we want to do what He wants us to do. His commandments are not hard for us to keep because we know how much He loves us, and we know He wouldn't tell us to do something that wasn't good for us. When He tells us not to do something, we should understand that it is for our own good to refrain from doing that because we know how much He loves us. We understand that by obeying Him, He is keeping us out of trouble.

> ...even though everything in the world is trying to lead us away from God, we know that our faith in Him is all that we need.

It's not burdensome for us to tithe because we know that when we put God first, He opens the windows of heaven and showers us with blessings beyond what we could ever imagine. It's not burdensome for us to give up drugs because we know what drugs do to us and to those we love. It's not burdensome to give up drunkenness because we know it is destroying our family. It's not burdensome for us to give up adultery because we know what it does to the family, how it destroys trust and ruins relationships.

The Bible says that our faith in the Lord is what will cause us to overcome the spirit of the world. And even though everything in the world is trying to lead us away from God, we know that our faith in Him is all that we need. Our faith in the Lord is more than enough. Without faith it's impossible to please God and that's why our spiritual enemy is always trying to steal our faith. He's always trying to make us think that God is not going to help us. He's always trying to make you think that you're such a failure that God won't help us. He's always trying to make us think that we've done too many sinful and hurtful things and now God's not going to help us. Satan is always trying to make us think we're not worthy to be blessed by God. But I tell you that the devil is a liar. You see, the enemy knows that when we have real faith and then put some action with it, nothing is impossible for us. That's why he's always trying to convince us that God's Word doesn't work. He's always trying to get us to be impatient. He's always trying to get us to put the Word

> *You see, the enemy knows that when we have real faith and then put some action with it, nothing is impossible for us.*

down and begin to compromise. You see, my faith in the Lord is what's going to cause me to overcome the spirit of anti-Christ that's all around me. It's my faith in Him that will help me overcome the world and all the negativity that surrounds me every day. Faith will help me overcome the spirit of failure that is always trying to steal my future and my destiny.

God has a wonderful plan for us, but in one way or

another, the enemy is always trying to cause us to live under a spirit of failure so we will not fulfill our destiny. When God's children lived in Egypt, they lived under a spirit of failure, and they lived under that failure because they would not put God first. They lived in destruction because they would not honor God. God promised His people that as long as they were careful to do all He commanded, they would be blessed, highly favored and empowered to prosper.

> *As long as I have the Lord in my life and use my faith in Him, the spirit of failure cannot stop me.*

But the children of God did their own thing, and they would not develop their faith in the Lord. Instead they worshipped other gods. God then allowed them to live in destruction and slavery for four hundred years because they would not turn from their sin. It wasn't an accident they fell into slavery. God allowed slavery to overtake them to teach them a lesson. You will become a slave to the thing you worship, whether it's drugs or booze or sex. That's why God says you must put Him first in every part of your life.

As long as I have the Lord in my life and use my faith in Him, the spirit of failure cannot stop me. As long as I seek first the kingdom of God and His righteousness, the Bible tells me, everything I need will eventually be added unto me in due season. It may not happen today, but it's coming my way. I declare it with my own mouth.

Because God's people would not use their faith in the Lord, He allowed them to live in sickness, in poverty, and in a spirit of failure. No matter who you are, if you refuse to put God first, if you do your thing, the same thing will happen to you. Once the children

> *Once the children of God cried out for deliverance from their slavery, God began the process of bringing them out of their bondage.*

of God cried out for deliverance from their slavery, God began the process of bringing them out of their bondage. When He brought them out of their bondage, He took them out into the wilderness because the wilderness was the pathway into the Promised Land. Don't be mad at God because He saved you and now you're going through the wilderness, because it's in the wilderness that God is teaching you the fight of faith. He's teaching you to have faith in Him, and He's changing you. In your wilderness experience, He will make you a better person. It's in the wilderness that God's teaching you that He can do anything but fail.

I know that some people think it's okay to smoke pot once in a while, but that's why God has them in the wilderness. I know some saved folk think it's okay to date the unbelievers down at work, but that's why God has them in the wilderness. You see, God will find a way of getting your attention before it's over. Anytime God is working in your life, He'll lead you into the wilderness. If you are in the wilderness, you need to know that God is working in your life. When God is working in your life, He'll talk to you about your faith. He'll talk to you about the direction you're going. He'll talk to you about the friends that you're keeping. He'll talk to you about the way that you are living your life.

> *Once the children of God came out of Egypt, they got discouraged because things did not happen fast enough for them. Are you a person who gets really discouraged when your plans don't happen fast enough?*

Once the children of God came out of Egypt, they got discouraged because things did not happen fast enough for them. Are you a person who gets really discouraged when your plans don't happen fast enough? Most of us tend to start complaining or we get negative if things don't happen fast enough. The problem with being negative and complaining is that God takes it personally. It makes Him think that you don't have faith in Him, and it makes Him think that you don't trust Him. I know you don't think that complaining or being negative reveals a lack of faith, but God thinks it does. You see, you can complain about your job if you want to, but I'm just going to be thankful that I've got a job. I'm going to say, "Lord, I'm not going to complain about this car I have; I'm going to be thankful that I have a car."

The children of Israel became greatly discouraged in the wilderness because they lived in difficult situations. There's something inside all of us that becomes discouraged when things are difficult or when we have to struggle too much. Anytime we struggle in our marriage, we get disappointed. Anytime we struggle with our finances, we get disappointed, but God wants you to have faith in Him because it's your faith in Him that's going to cause you to overcome whatever it is that you're going through.

The flesh wants everything to go easy. The flesh doesn't want to come in early before the church service and pray. The flesh doesn't even want to come to church at all. The flesh doesn't want to tithe, and the flesh sure enough doesn't want to make any sacrifices. The flesh wants to quit when the going gets tough, but as we grow up in Christ, we learn to say, "God I'm going to trust in You for myself. I know You made me to be an overcomer, and I am not going to live under a spirit of failure all of my life."

Even when your journey is difficult, you have to learn to keep speaking faith out of your mouth. You have to learn to keep trusting God no matter what you see, and that's why you must keep coming to church even though you're disappointed. You are using your faith, you're trusting in God no matter what you're going through.

But since you're determined to hang on to your faith, you have to be careful of who your friends are because birds of a feather flock together. You have to be careful of the things you're saying because "Death and life are in the power of the tongue; and those that love it will eat its fruit" (Proverbs 18:21). You're going to be justified or condemned by the words you say, so you have to guard the words in your mouth if you're going to overcome the spirit of failure that has been brought down from generation to generation. "Trust in the Lord with all of your heart, lean not unto your own understanding" (Proverbs 3:5).

> *You have to be careful of the things you're saying because "Death and life are in the power of the tongue;*

I will not live under a spirit of failure all my life. If God be for me, who can be against me? I may be disappointed, but I will trust in Him. Even if on the inside I'm not trusting in Him, I'm saying with my mouth I will trust in Him. Trust is an act of my will. Things may be rougher than I want them to be, but I will trust in Him. I may be going through hell and high water and not understand why He's letting this happen to me, but I will trust in Him. I will speak faith out of my mouth. I will trust in God. I will have faith in God. I will not let the devil steal my faith by talking negative.

> It takes faith to forgive people who have hurt you. Yo u may think it's a forgiveness issue, but it's not. In reality it's nothing but a faith issue.

It takes faith to forgive people who have hurt you. You may think it's a forgiveness issue, but it's not. In reality it's nothing but a faith issue. Unforgiveness is going by what you see. Forgiveness is walking by faith, trusting that God is going to work it out even though you don't see how it can work out. It's a faith issue. I'm going to keep my faith because I'm going to forgive you, I'm going to let it go, and I'm going to get it all behind me.

It's my faith that's going to cause me to overcome the spirit of failure that's come against my life. "Faith cometh by hearing and hearing by the Word of God" (Romans 10:17). I have to be in church every time the doors open. I know you think you can just come to church whenever you want to, and that's fine. But I have to be in church every time I can get through the doors because I have to do what I can to get built up in my faith. That's because it's my faith that's going to help me overcome the spirit of failure that's trying to get a hold of me.

The writer of Hebrews said in chapter 10, "Do not throw away your confidence which has a great reward." The devil's plan is for you to be so discouraged that you throw away your confidence in God. He wants you to get so discouraged that you say, "Oh, what's the use in trying."

Make no mistake about it, faith is not something you receive by joining the church. It's not something you receive by shaking the preacher's hand; faith comes by hearing and hearing the Word of God.

Make no mistake about it, faith is not something you receive by joining the church. It's not something you receive by shaking the preacher's hand; faith comes by hearing and hearing the Word of God. It comes by having a relationship with Him and putting God first. Even if I come from a family that has always lived under a spirit of failure, I can break that thing by putting God first and operating in faith.

It's through my faith in the Lord that I will overcome all the failure of my past. It's through my faith that I will overcome the sickness that's trying to kill me. It's through my faith that I will overcome all of the poverty that's run in my family. Use your faith and put God first. Then watch what God does in your life.

I thank God for grace because grace gives me another chance, a second chance and a third chance and a fourth chance. I thank God for His grace. But grace by itself is not enough to help me overcome the spirit of failure. It's going to take my faith in the Lord to cause me to overcome the spirit of failure. It seems like everything in this world is trying to bring me down. Everything is trying to lead me away from my faith in the Lord. But by my faith in the Lord I'm going to overcome every part of my life, every obstacle, and all the failures of my past.

> *The enemy forms all kinds of weapons against you, but they can't take you out because God already said they couldn't take you out.*

The Bible says in Isaiah 54 that no weapon formed against a true believer shall prosper. And every tongue that rises in judgment shall be condemned for this is the heritage of the servants of the Lord. If you are a servant of the Lord then no amount of trouble can stop you. I didn't say trouble wouldn't come; I just said that trouble couldn't stop you.

The enemy forms all kinds of weapons against you, but they can't take you out because God already said they couldn't take you out. Faith says I may be going through something really bad, but "All things work together for the good of those that love Him and are called according to His purpose" (Romans 8:28). The enemy sends his fiery darts against me, he causes people to come against me, and talk

about me, but God is going to close the mouth of all my critics before it's over. That's what faith is all about.

...genuine faith will always take you somewhere.

Since you're a servant of the Lord, no disease can stop you. No disease can defeat you. Since you're a servant of the Lord, no amount of family trouble can defeat you. That's what faith in Him is all about. There are so many times when we all feel like quitting, but it's our faith in the Lord that causes us to keep going. It's our faith that causes us to refuse to quit. It's our faith in Him that says I'm never going to back up, I'm never going to give up, I am too legit to quit.

It may appear that your faith is not working, and it may look like God is not listening. It may appear as though you are not going anywhere with your life, but genuine faith will always take you somewhere. Sometimes it will take you into the fiery furnace. You see, the three Hebrew boys were thrown into the fire, and their faith in the Lord so angered Nebuchadnezzar that he had the furnace heated seven times hotter than normal. But, it was faith that caused the fourth man [Christ] to show up in the midst of their trial. I'm telling you that faith will make a way where there is no way. He's an on-time God, yes He is.

I'll tell you something else about faith. Genuine faith must be tested. I know you don't want to hear that part, but it's true. Sometimes genuine faith will take you into the fiery furnace. Genuine faith may take you into the lion's den. Genuine faith will take you into the valley of the shadow of death, but that's when you have to use your faith and say, "I will fear no evil, for thou art with me." Genuine faith will go through difficult circumstances, but that's when you trust in the Lord. My faith may be tested by trials and tribulations, but I'm going to trust in Him. I am telling you that my faith in the Lord will cause me to be victorious before it's over. I may have been given a bad report, but I know that it's going to turn around before it's over.

When the bottom is falling out in your life, there is one thing that nobody can take from you. They can take your house, they can take your car, they can take your husband or your wife, but there is one thing they cannot take from you, and that is your faith in the Lord Jesus Christ. When everything fails you, it's your faith that will take you to the other side. When people have walked out of your life, and you're all by yourself, just keep trusting God, because nobody can take your faith in the Lord from you. Before it's over, God is going to turn everything around.

> *...just keep trusting God, because nobody can take your faith in the Lord from you. Before it's over, God is going to turn everything around.*

The woman with the issue of blood had faith in the Lord. She was sick for twelve long years and had gone through much at the hands of physicians. She spent all that she had and only grew worse. You see, it's one thing to be sick for twelve hours, but it's another to be sick for twelve years. She was sick for twelve long years, but the Bible tells us that she kept saying, "If I can just touch Him, I shall get well. I'm going through a whole lot, but if I can just touch Him, I shall get well. It looks like I'm going to die, but I know if I can just touch Him, I shall get well."

You see death and life are in the power of the tongue. She kept saying, "if I can but touch Him, I shall get well." She was broke, busted, and disgusted, but she kept saying, "My faith is in the Lord." Folk had turned their backs on her, but she kept saying it. Religious traditions said, "You keep away from Him," but she kept saying it. They said, "Stay locked up in your house woman, you better not come out," but she kept saying it.

You have to make up your mind that no matter what you're going through you're going to keep speaking faith. I don't care what it looks like, I don't care what people are saying. You have to keep saying, "My faith is in the Lord, and He's going to bring me out. It may not look good, but the devil can't have my faith. "I shall get well. I'm not going to be broke forever."

Let me tell you, she pressed through all of the obstacles in her life. Real faith will press. Real faith doesn't say, "Well, if it's God's will, go ahead and help me." Real faith says, "I shall get my healing." Real faith will press. This woman was determined to reach out and touch

> *That's what God wants you to do today. He wants you to press through all your fears. Press through all your discouragement. Press through...*

Jesus. That's what God wants you to do today. He wants you to press through all your fears. Press through all your discouragement. Press through all the gossip that's been told about you. Press through all of the bankruptcies. Press through all of the divorces. Press through it all, and say, "I know if I can just touch Him, I shall be well."

Paul said in 2 Timothy 4:7, "I fought the good fight, I've finished the course. I kept the faith." Everything you're going through today is about your faith. You think it's about who you married. You think it's about your financial condition. It's all about your faith. It's about finishing the things that God called you to do. The enemy causes people to come against you so he can steal your faith. He brings negative folk around you to steal your faith.

Whatever is born of God overcomes the world. Whatever is born of God will overcome the spirit of failure that has attached itself to your life and to your family's life. In fact, your faith in the Lord is so supernatural, it doesn't even make any sense sometimes. In fact, real faith will look at the impossible and say, "I don't believe you. I don't believe my children are going to hell. I don't believe the devil can kill me. I don't believe I'm going to be broke all my life. I don't believe I'm going to live under the spirit of failure." Real faith talks. Real faith speaks. Real faith says, "This is my year. 'Greater is He that lives in me than he that lives in the world.' God is turning everything around. I may be tested, but I'm coming out of this thing. I will not live under the spirit of failure. I'm walking by faith and God is turning this thing around."

You're closer to your victory than you think. You are stronger than you think. You've got more faith than you think, and you're coming out of this thing. There's greatness inside you, and it's only a matter of time until God turns everything around.

No More Leftovers

14

THE POWER OF YOUR WORDS

We live in a society that's filled with stress. Life doesn't always turn out the way we have it planned. Many times life leaves us depressed, and any time we are disappointed, depression tries to come in. Whenever we have losses in our lives, we can feel great discouragement. A bad report can leave us feeling discouraged. Many times life has a way of crushing us and bringing us to our knees.

There is something inside each of us that thinks, "Well, if we had more money, then we would be happy." We think if we just had a bigger house, then we would be happy. If we had a nicer car, then we would be happy. We tend to think if we had more things in our lives, then we would have more joy. But it's not true.

You can love God with all of your heart and still get discouraged. You can serve God and still get depressed. Elijah became so depressed that he wanted to die after his ministry suffered a rapid reversal. He begged God to take his life. Have you ever been to a point in your life where you still loved God, but things were just so hard and so painful you didn't even know if life was worth living? Jonah did. He got to the point that he cried out, "O Lord, take, I beseech thee, my life from me; for it is better for me to die than to live" (Jonah 4:3).

> Even the disciples became greatly discouraged because of the persecutions in their lives. Have you known the discouragement of persecution on your job?

Even the disciples became greatly discouraged because of the persecutions in their lives. Have you known the discouragement of persecution on your job? Have you known the discouragement of giving and giving in ministry, parenting, or care giving without rest, recreation, or time away? Caring for people and carrying their burdens can wipe you out and cause you to become discouraged.

Life is always full of hardships, difficulties, stress, and even failures. That's why Jesus said, "Don't let life get you down because I have already overcome on your behalf" (John 16:33). When the children of Israel were in Egypt they were slaves. They had been abused and life had beaten them down. As a result they had a hard time believing God. They had a hard time walking in faith. When people have an abusive past, they have a hard time walking in faith because they don't feel worthy. They have a poor self-image and often have a negative view of life.

Even when the children of Israel were finally freed from slavery, they still struggled almost all the time. They were negative gossipers who constantly murmured and complained about their lives, their fears, Moses, and even God. They were backbiters, living under a spirit

> *Even when the children of Israel were finally freed from slavery, they still struggled almost all the time.*

of failure, and always struggling with depression. You would think that they'd be grateful for their freedom from slavery, but they complained bitterly about every hardship, real or imaginary. God got so tired of their negative attitudes and complaining that He told them they were going to live and die in the wilderness, never to receive the promises of God, nor enter the Promised Land.

The lesson for us is this: Once God has brought you

out of your past and out of your slavery to sin, He expects you to be grateful and quit complaining. He expects you to exhibit faith and to start speaking faith out of your mouth.

> *I'm telling you, if you are doing nothing but going in circles in your walk with the Lord and in your life, you have to stop and look at yourself and say, "Wait a minute. What kind of report do I have in my own mouth?"*

God sent twelve spies into the Promised Land, and ten of them came back with a negative report. God heard the report, and He called it an evil report. I find it interesting that God called a negative report an evil report. Remember, He provided food and water in the wilderness. And He didn't even let their shoes wear out for forty years in the wilderness and for forty years all they did was walk around in a circle.

I'm telling you, if you are doing nothing but going in circles in your walk with the Lord and in your life, you have to stop and look at yourself and say, "Wait a minute. What kind of report do I have in my own mouth?" For forty years they did nothing but go in circles, and still, God loved them. It's interesting that God loved them and took care of them, but He never let them progress. He never let them go into the Promised Land. They lived under a spirit of failure all the rest of their lives because of their murmuring and backbiting.

There is a principle in the kingdom of God that says you have to have a praise report when it looks bad. There is a principle in the kingdom of God that says you have to learn to worship God while you are in the wilderness or you can't get out of the wilderness. God says that we have to use faith in Him if we are going to please Him. It's all about walking by faith and not by sight.

> *There is a principle in the kingdom of God that says you have to learn to worship God while you are in the wilderness or you can't get out of the wilderness.*

The children of Israel stayed in the wilderness for forty years because they wouldn't change their attitude. They kept saying, "Well, we had it better in Egypt, let's go back to Egypt; it's better there than here. Did he bring us out here to let us die?" God loved them, but He let them die in their depression. He loved them, but He let them die broke. He loved them, but He let them die under a spirit of failure. They never fulfilled their destiny because they lived in doubt and unbelief all of their lives. They kept saying things like, "Why did God let us go through this trouble? Why won't He bring me out? Why did He lead me into this miserable place?"

You'll never get healed as long as you say, "I don't know why God won't heal me." You'll never get that great job until you stop saying, "I don't know why God won't help me get a good job." You are never going to find a mate as long as you're complaining and murmuring and backbiting. You're never going to get that house until you start proclaiming, "You watch what God does for me!" I wonder how many of you are saying, "Why did God give me this miserable wife or husband? Why did God give me this lousy job? Why did God let this happen to me?"

> You will always live under a spirit of failure until you make up your mind to say what God says and not what your emotions tell you to say.

So many people are like the children of Israel. They look at their situation, and they start complaining. They start speaking about the things they see. They talk negatively until depression overtakes them. All they would have to do is what God said and have a good report instead of a bad report. You will always live under a spirit of failure until you make up your mind to say what God says and not what your emotions tell you to say. If you say, "I hate my job" enough times, it won't be long until you either get fired or you quit. If you say, "I don't love my spouse anymore," it won't be long until you'll be sleeping in somebody else's bed.

If you are tired of living under a spirit of failure and depression, you have to change the things you are saying. If you're tired of living in the wilderness, you have to change the things you're saying. While Jonah was in the pit of the great fish's stomach, he finally said, "God, I will pay my vows to you, and I have made up my mind to put on a heart of thanksgiving" (Jonah 2:9). You may be in the pit, but you have to thank Him anyhow. Quit talking about your problems. You

> *You don't have to be a drug addict for the devil to defeat you. All you have to do is be a complainer.*

may be in the wilderness, but you have to learn to put on a heart of thanksgiving while you're there. You have to thank the Lord for all He has done. You have to thank Him for all He's going to do.

You don't have to be a drug addict for the devil to defeat you. All you have to do is be a complainer. The children of Israel complained so much that God sent snakes into their camp and killed many of them. I'm telling you that complaining opens the door for the snakes to come in. Complaining opens the door for the devil, the enemy of your soul, to come in and steal everything you have. He'll steal your joy, he'll steal your peace of mind, he'll steal your family, and he'll steal your shout. When you are negative, it shows God that you don't trust Him. When you complain, it tells God that you are not walking by faith. By faith we must say things we don't necessarily feel.

The Bible says, "With the heart man believes resulting in righteousness and with the mouth he confesses resulting in salvation" (Romans 10:10). In other words, everything you receive in the kingdom of God comes by confessing it first. You cannot get saved without confessing it first. The reason some of you don't feel saved is because you won't confess Jesus as Lord with your own mouth. You will never receive healing, unless you start confessing it first. You will never lose your weight, unless you start confessing it first. You'll never stop smoking, unless you start confessing it first. You're never going to live in divine health, unless you start confessing it first.

> ...everything you receive in the kingdom of God comes by confessing it first.

For years I confessed that I lived in divine health even when I was sick. And through the years God began to show me how to exercise, showed me how to eat right, showed me how to change some of the things in my diet so I can live in divine health.

We all know that attitude determines altitude. You can

watch your own bad attitude change when you start speaking faith. You will never overcome the spirit of failure until you change your words and speak a good report. James said that the tongue is an unruly member of your body. He said if you contain your tongue, you can change the direction of your life (James 3).

> *James said that the tongue is like a rudder of a ship, it will guide you to safety, or it will guide you to destruction.*

You're walking around feeling depressed when all you had to do was change some of the things you're saying. I'm talking about a discipline in your life. I'm not going to speak whatever just pops into my head. James said that the tongue is like a rudder of a ship, it will guide you to safety, or it will guide you to destruction. Jesus said it's not what enters a man mouth that defiles him, it's what comes out, and you are justified or condemned by your own words (Matthew 15:11).

The author in Psalms said the tongue is the pen of a ready writer. In other words, the things you say will determine your future. The things you say are written in the spirit. The things you say will either increase or decrease your faith.

Joshua and Caleb were the only two who had a good report in their mouths. They were the only two of all the Israelites that God delivered from Egypt who went into the

Promised Land. All the others died, but God kept Caleb and Joshua alive because of the good report they gave after spying on the land. They are a model for us today. If we'll learn to have a good report in our mouths in spite of what we're going through, God says we'll receive all the blessings that He has promised to us.

> Proverbs 15:23 says, "A man has joy by the answer that's in his mouth." The things you say determine whether you walk in joy or walk in depression.

Proverbs 15:23 says, "A man has joy by the answer that's in his mouth." The things you say determine whether you walk in joy or walk in depression. No matter who we are, we all get down, and we all feel discouraged from time to time. The Word of God is plain and says, you can have joy by speaking joy out of your mouth (Proverbs 15:23). You can have joy that's off the hook.

I can be going through a difficult time in my life, but when I begin to proclaim the Word of God, something happens inside me when I say, "The joy of the Lord is my strength" (Nehemiah 8:10). What I'm really doing is bringing a faith report, I'm bringing a good report in the middle of my wilderness. The joy of the Lord is my strength!

So I say with my mouth, "Greater is He that lives in me,

than He that lives in the world" (John 4:4). Well, how do you feel? "My God is causing all things to work together to the good of those that love Him and are called according to His purpose" (Romans 8:28). What am I doing? I'm bringing a good report, I'm bringing a faith report rather than what God calls an evil report. If you want to overcome the spirit of failure in your life, you have to start bragging on God. If you want to have joy that's off the hook, you have to speak crazy faith when you don't feel it. I'm trying to get you to say things with your own mouth, because that will eventually get you going in the right direction.

> *You have to brag on God when it looks like He's forgotten you. You have to brag on Him when it looks like nothing is working out.*

You have to brag on God when it looks like He's forgotten you. You have to brag on Him when it looks like nothing is working out. You have to brag on Him when it looks like all has been lost. You may be in the wilderness today, but the wilderness is a test to find out if you get to go into the Promised Land or not. If you're the kind of person who just speaks whatever pops into your mind, you are going to live in the wilderness all of your life.

When you walk by faith, you can't go by how you feel, even when your mind says you are never going to be happy again. You have to guard the words in your mouth. Even when you feel as though you'll never achieve your goals, you have to say, "I will achieve my goals. I can do all things through Christ who strengthens me. I can overcome the spirit of failure. I will be happy in my life."

Jesus said, "Whoever says to this mountain, be thou removed, and be thou cast into the sea; and does not doubt in his heart, but believes those things he says, will have whatever he says" (Mark 11:23). In that passage, the word "believe" is only used one time, but the word "says" is used three times. You don't need a lot of faith, but you do need to speak faith, and speak it, and speak it, and speak it.

> Jesus said, "Whoever says to this mountain, be thou removed, and be thou cast into the sea; and does not doubt in his heart, but believes those things he says, will have whatever he says" (Mark 11:23).

Did you know that life will steal your joy? Even those who live in your house will try and steal your joy. But it's you who decides whether you walk in joy or depression. Quit living your life by how you feel and start having a good report in your mouth. No matter how bad things may look you have to have a good report. You have to speak to your valley of dry bones. You have to talk to your giants. You have to call things that be not as though they were. "Death and life are in the power of the tongue: and those who love it will eat its fruit" (Proverbs 18:21). In other words, Solomon said that you will end up eating the fruit of everything that you say.

Start saying, "My giants are coming down. My God is working everything out. I may be in a storm today, but this too shall pass. No weapon formed against me shall prosper (Isaiah 54:17). Many are the afflictions of the righteous, but the Lord shall deliver me out of them all (Psalm 34:19). I am more than a conqueror through Christ Jesus that loves me" (Romans 8:37).

Stop saying it's too hard for me. Stop saying it's too hard to quit smoking, it's too hard to lose weight, it's too hard being a Christian. My Bible says the way of the transgressor is hard, not the way of the believer. Start saying, "I can do all things through Christ." You have to know that God is looking for those who will have a good report in their mouth. He's looking for somebody to put on a heart of thanksgiving while in the wilderness. It's not a sin to think negatively, just don't speak it out of your mouth. David said, "Oh magnify the Lord with me" (Psalm 34:3). He didn't say magnify your problems. He didn't say talk about your giants;

He said tell your giants how big your God is. Begin to magnify your God, and tell everybody how big God is.

The reason the devil always tempts us in the area of complaining is because he knows as long as we do, we'll live under a spirit of failure. He knows that the more you talk about anything, the bigger it gets. The more you talk about your problem and how bad it is, the worse it gets. The more you magnify God and talk about His goodness and His mercy that endures forever, the more your faith rises up and the bigger God gets in your life.

> *Your words are like a bit in a horse's mouth that's going to guide you one direction or the other. Start saying, "My God's meeting all my needs"*

"Well, Bishop, no matter how hard I try, I just can't seem to get ahead." You better be quiet. You better change the things you're saying, because death and life are in the power of the tongue. Your words are like a bit in a horse's mouth that's going to guide you one direction or the other. Start saying, "My God's meeting all my needs" (Philippians 4:19). What the devil meant for evil, God's going to turn it for good. It's only a matter of time until God turns it around.

You see, when your children aren't serving the Lord the way they should, you have to confess, "Me and my house shall be saved, the devil can't have my children. He may have them right now, but he can't have them forever. The Blood of Jesus is over my children."

When you're going through the biggest test of your life, you have to confess that your best days are still ahead. In due season, I'm going to reap a harvest if I don't grow weary. My day is coming, and my breakthrough is coming.

"Let them shout for joy, and be glad, that favor my righteous cause: yea, let them say continually, Let the Lord be magnified, which hath pleasure in the prosperity of his servant." (Psalm 35:27)

> *When you're going through the biggest test of your life, you have to confess that your best days are still ahead.*

There are several things I want you to see here. One is, you're waiting for something to change in your life so you can be happy. We are all that way, but God says you don't need the preacher to lay hands on you so you can have joy. He says, let them shout for joy. You can act dignified if you want to, but sometimes my shout is nothing more than me saying, "God, I'm reaching up for some joy that I don't have." Psalm 35:27 says, "Let them shout for joy and rejoice." That's an act of your will. I can't do it for you. Your spouse can't do it for you. "Well, preacher, it's just not my personality." This doesn't have a thing to do with your personality. This has to do with whether you're going to obey the Word of God or not. It's time to change the words of your mouth and go into the promises of God.

15

LET IT GO

Jesus said that when you are praying, make sure that you forgive everyone who has ever treated you poorly or hurt you. He said that if you don't forgive them, your Heavenly Father won't forgive you. God takes this forgiveness principle very seriously.

Preachers talk a lot about their favorite sins. They talk a lot about sins of the flesh, but none of those sins are as serious to God as an unforgiving heart. When you fail to forgive others, the Bible says that you are in big trouble with God.

The Word of God is very plain. You will always live under a spirit of failure if you refuse to forgive those who have hurt you. You will never live an overcoming life as long as you hold on to the bad things that have happened to you.

The Bible tells us that unforgiveness is part of the very nature of our spiritual enemy while forgiveness is an essential part of God's nature. And if you are born again, God expects you to forgive because you are created in God's image (Genesis 1:27). If you don't develop a forgiving nature, you will always live under a spirit of failure that will continue until you make up your mind to obey the Word of God.

> Anytime you get your feelings hurt, you have to decide whether you will release the offender or whether you will hang on to what the person has done.

Anytime you get your feelings hurt, you have to decide whether you will release the offender or whether you will hang on to what the person has done. If you think about someone, and that memory causes you to get a bad attitude, or your blood starts to boil, you have unforgiveness issues that you will have to deal with regarding that person.

If you give someone the silent treatment, you are still hanging on to a hurt or some other issue. Anytime you won't let somebody off of the hook, it's a sign of unforgiveness. Before you gave your life to the Lord you were hateful, and you got an attitude when people hurt you. But now that you are born again, the Lord expects you to rise above your flesh.

He expects you to grow up in Christ and become mature. Maturity is marked by behavior that is calm, reasonable, and fair-minded. Mature people will do the "right thing", even though their flesh may be telling them differently.

Often you'll hear people, sometimes even Christians, say, "Well, I'll forgive you, but I'm not going to forget it." That's immaturity and unforgiveness. It's a way of holding people hostage for the things they've done to us. It's a means of trying to make someone pay for offending you.

Unforgiveness ties you to the person that hurt you with an invisible cord. When you don't forgive someone, you have to think about

> *Unforgiveness ties you to the person that hurt you with an invisible cord.*

the person all the time. Unforgiveness makes you a slave to the person that hurt you. Why would you want to give people that much power over you? On the other hand, if you will release them, then God can release you. You may hate somebody, but because of your unforgiving spirit, you will be tied to them for years. You are becoming their prisoner through your own willful act of refusing to forgive and nourishing the memories you keep replaying in your mind.

Somebody may have abused you in the past, but because you won't forgive them and let it go, you may be tormented with those thoughts and memories all of your life. Let me tell you something, life is too short to have all this mental and emotional baggage beating you up day after day.

Sometimes you just have to say, "I'm hurting, but I will let it go. I don't understand why you did this to me, but I will let it go. I can't be carrying you with me all of my life, so I will let it go."

> Sometimes you just have to say, "I'm hurting, but I will let it go. I don't understand why you did this to me, but I will let it go.

Jesus told a story in Matthew 18:23-35 about a certain king who had a slave that owed him millions of dollars, but because the man had no way of repaying the debt, the king forgave him what he owed. The same slave had a friend that owed him a few dollars. He grabbed his friend and began to choke him, saying, "You better repay me the money you owe me or else." But the man couldn't repay the few dollars he owed, so the slave had the friend thrown into prison. When the king heard what the slave did, he went to the man and said, "I forgave you of an impossible debt that you couldn't repay, but you wouldn't forgive another of a small debt he couldn't pay. Now I'm going to make you pay." And Jesus said, "My Heavenly Father will do the same thing to you if you don't forgive your fellow man from your heart."

Your debt against heaven is so great that you could never repay it, but God forgives you anyway. Now when you find out that somebody did something to you, God says it's only a little thing, so you better just let it go. Jesus said if you don't forgive others, you will be turned over to the tormentors. You see, unforgiveness will cause you to lose sleep. It will cause you to hate and will eat at your insides. It can cause you to live under a spirit of failure for years. Unforgiveness can even cause you to try to get even with somebody, but God says vengeance is His area, not ours (Romans 12:19).

> *In the kingdom of God, you have to forgive others if you expect God to forgive you.*

In the kingdom of God, you have to forgive others if you expect God to forgive you. Jesus said, "Give and it shall be given back to you. Good measure, pressed down, shaken together and running over" (Luke 6:38). But He wasn't talking just about money. He was talking about attitudes. He was talking about the way you treat others. He was stating, the way you give to others is the way God gives back to you. When you don't totally release others, then God doesn't totally release you.

You have a problem with your mother-in-law. You have a problem with your brother or your sister. You have a problem with your boss. You have a problem with your neighbor. You have a problem now with your pastor, you have a problem with your church, and you wonder why God won't heal you. You wonder why God won't bring a breakthrough in your business. You wonder why God won't bring you a miracle in your life. But the truth of the matter is, God can't do anything for you because of your attitude and because of the heavens being all bound up around you. You're sick, and you can't get well because you won't forgive others. You catch more colds than anybody else, and unforgiveness weakens your immune system so you catch everything.

You've been to the doctor, and he can't find anything wrong with you. He's run all kinds of tests and doesn't know what to do. But the truth of the matter is, it's unforgiveness that's binding everything around you and making you sick, so sick you can't get well. You have a chip on your shoulder everywhere you go, and you have a problem with everybody, and now God has a problem with you.

If you don't forgive your parents, you'll grow up and become just like them. You see, you may not want to forgive them, but now that you're born again, you don't have to go by how you feel anymore. You can do all things through Christ who strengthens you (Philippians 4:13). You can forgive them through Christ, but in the natural you can't, because your flesh doesn't want to let go of what they did. I don't know about you, but I'm tired of living under the spirit of failure and of being in the wilderness. I'm ready for God to do a new thing, and I'm ready to go into my Promised Land. I'm ready to be blessed.

There are certain types of people who always struggle with forgiving themselves. And it's almost always because they have a hard time forgiving others. Because they can't forgive others, they can't even receive forgiveness for

> *There are certain types of people who always struggle with forgiving themselves. And it's almost always because they have a hard time forgiving others.*

themselves. When you don't forgive others or when you don't release others, you can't be released yourself. And you always reap what you sow (Galatians 6:7). Whatever you give out is what you get back. If you want to be able to forgive yourself of all the things you've done wrong, you have to forgive others of what they've do to you.

The truth is, forgiveness is nothing more than an obedience issue and a faith issue. It takes real faith to forgive folk that have hurt you. It takes faith to release others and believe God is going to take care of everything on your behalf. But the Bible has already told you, "The just shall live by faith" (Galatians 3:11).

The Bible says that faith worketh by love (Galatians 5:6). If you don't know how to love others, your faith won't even work. If you can't release somebody from what they've done, how can you expect God to release you? The Bible says that your faith will not operate properly unless you are walking in love. Maybe that's why you don't see that miracle in your life.

> *When you forgive people who don't deserve it, you are proving that you are a person of faith.*

When you forgive people who don't deserve it, you are proving that you are a person of faith. When you forgive undeserving people, you are proving that you love the Lord because the Word says, "If I diligently obey the Lord my God, He'll command the blessing on me" (Deuteronomy 28:1,8).

If you keep going from failure to failure, you'd better stop and look at your life, examine yourself, find out why that cloud is over you because God promised He would bless you if you obeyed Him.

You don't have to feel forgiving to forgive. Faith is not about feelings, it's about obedience. You can't help how you feel, but you can help how you react. You can't change where you've been, but you can change where you're going.

As long as I obey the Word of God, I will be blessed, highly favored, and empowered to prosper. That's why I have to drop the charges against you. I know you're guilty, and God knows you're guilty, but I'm determined that I'm going to drop the charges. So, quit living your life on how you feel. Faith is a decision, not a feeling. If you go by how you feel, you'll never forgive anybody. You'll never release people from the things they've done to you. It's time to quit drinking from that cup of bitterness and pain.

> *Faith is a decision, not a feeling. If you go by how you feel, you'll never forgive anybody.*

I'm talking about putting your arms around that man who hurt you instead of avoiding him. I'm talking about making up your mind to let go of what she has said and done. The Bible says, "give no place to the devil" (Ephesians 4:27), but when you have unforgiveness in your heart, you are giving the devil a place in your life. When you have unforgiveness in your heart, and you won't let people go, what you've said is, "Hey, mister devil, come on in and take everything you want." Unforgiveness will cause you to fail faster than anything else you can do.

So who are you avoiding? Oh, I know you didn't blow up, you kept your cool, you've got your temper under control. But who are you avoiding? God can't bring you a new mate until you forgive your ex-spouse. You keep praying, "Oh, God, bring me a husband. Oh, God, bring me a wife."

And God says, "I can't bring you another one until you forgive the last one I brought you.

If you're tired of living under a spirit of failure, you have to forgive some folks. If you want to go on with your life, you have to get that chip off of your shoulder,

Sometimes we have to release broken relationships before we can move on to new relationships. Sometimes we have to let go of old things before we can move on to new things. God can't answer your prayers until you quit talking about the things "he" or "she" did to you. The Lord can't do a thing for you until you quit trying to turn the kids against your ex-spouse.

If you're tired of living under a spirit of failure, you have to forgive some folks. If you want to go on with your life, you have to get that chip off of your shoulder, let some things go, and act as though it never happened. It's a waste of time to dwell on things people have done to you. It's a waste of time to blame your parents for the things they did or did not do for you. It's time to drop the charges.

Jesus prayed, "Father, forgive us our debts as we forgive

our debtors" (Matthew 6:12). We have to go to God for forgiveness, but as we go to Him, we have to let go of everything people have done against us. If we expect God to forgive us our debts, then we have to forgive people their debts toward us.

Jesus was abused, mistreated, and beaten. Soldiers hit Him, pulled out His beard, spit on Him, and rejected Him. Then they nailed Him to the cross, and as He hung there, He said, "Father, forgive them for they know not what they do" (Luke 23:34). Just like Jesus did, sometimes you simply need to look at folk and say quietly to yourself, "God, I just let it go. I know they have their own problems, but I just let it go. They don't know what they are doing Lord, so Father forgive them."

> *Just like Jesus did, sometimes you simply need to look at folk and say quietly to yourself, "God, I just let it go. I know they have their own problems, but I just let it go.*

God wants us to forgive others no matter what they've done to us. He wants us to release all the pain, cancel all the debts against others. You see, your miracle depends on what you do with this word today. You can break that generational curse over your family, but you have to forgive and let go of the past.

Jesus said in Matthew 7:1-2 that by the standard of

measurement you use regarding others, you will be measured yourself. That is, if you forgive a little bit, then you'll be forgiven a little bit. If you forgive a lot, then you'll be forgiven a lot. I don't know about you, but I need a lot of forgiveness.

> How can you call yourself a Christian if you hate somebody in your family? How can you call yourself a Christian if you hate someone down at work?

I need all of God's forgiveness in my life. And if I hold anything against you, I am actually holding myself hostage. You see, the way I treat you is the same way God ends up treating me. Do you really want God to treat you the way you treat others?

How can you call yourself a Christian if you hate somebody in your family? How can you call yourself a Christian if you hate someone down at work? How can you say, "I love God," and you hate a color of people or a culture of people? How can you call yourself a believer if you hate your ex?

Even if someone stole your childhood, you have to let it go and say, "God, I'm going to trust You, I'm going to pray for them, and I'm going to put it in Your hands." Release others and God will release you. Drop the charges against others and God will drop the charges against you. He may not take away all the memories of your past, but He'll take away all the pain of your past.

The reason God can't heal your marriage today is because you have allowed bitterness to come in. You see, bitterness has a way of eating you up. It has a way of destroying relationships. Bitterness brings a cloud over you so that everything you see is distorted. Bitterness can cause you to live under a spirit of failure all your life.

Job was a good man, but he lost everything he had. His friends were self-righteous church folk, and they began to spread rumors about Job. They began to say, "Hey, Job loved God, but he had all this sin in his life and that's why he went through all his trouble." Do you know how hurtful people can be? Even Christians can be more than you can take. But the Bible says Job began to pray for his friends, and when he did God began to turn everything around. If you want to watch God move in your life, start praying for people who have hurt you. I don't mean pray, "God, go get 'em; sick 'em Holy Ghost." I'm talking about, "God bless them. God forgive them. God meet all their needs. God turn everything around in their life."

The Bible says Job got back double for his trouble. If you want to see some restoration in your life, start praying for God to bless the people who have hurt you, and God will begin to bring back everything you've lost. Remember, the principle is: whatever you give out is what you get back. I serve a God of restoration, and I'm telling you that if God did it for me, He'll do it for you. He did it for Job, and He'll do it for you. Start praying for folk, and God will help you.

The reason your family is in a mess right now is because you won't let it go. You keep talking about what they did, but God wants you to just let it go and trust in Him.

You know the story about Joseph and how his brothers did him wrong and sold him into slavery. He landed at Potiphar's house for awhile, and Potiphar's wife lied about him. As a result, Joseph went to jail for twelve years for something he did not do. But Joseph forgave everybody in his life. If you'll begin to forgive folk who have lied about you, God will begin to turn things around. Joseph could have become bitter, but life got better because he kept on trusting God, and he kept on forgiving those who hurt him.

The reason your family is in a mess right now is because you won't let it go. You keep talking about what they did, but God wants you to just let it go and trust in Him. Start walking by faith instead of by sight. Sometimes it's your stinking pride that keeps you from saying, "I'm sorry."

If you'll humble yourself and begin to pray, God will begin to turn that difficult situation around. It's time to get your past behind you. It's time to forgive and forget. It's time to bury the past before the past buries you. It's time to let go of some things that people have done. It's time to say, "God, I trust you enough to put it in your hands."

Paul said, "Forget what lies behind and reach forward to what lies ahead" (Philippians 3:13). You can't change what people have done to you, so you might as well let it go and trust God. Forgive others, and God will forgive you.

> *The failures in your life are the result of decisions you have made, but that doesn't mean you have to stay there.*

You are where you are because of choices you have made. The failures in your life are the result of decisions you have made, but that doesn't mean you have to stay there. It doesn't mean that you can't get everything turned around in your life.

Everything starts with forgiveness. "God, forgive me, I have failed you, and now I must forgive others." If you don't understand that principle, you'll never see a breakthrough in your life. You'll never see a miracle in your life. You'll live under a spirit of failure all of your life.

"God, you were right and I was wrong. Now I forgive those that have hurt me." Admitting your sin and doing so quickly is one of the key principles in the Christian life. I know people who have made so many mistakes you would think that God wouldn't do anything for them. But they were quick to repent, they were quick to forgive, and God has done miracles in their lives.

This is not an easy teaching. But it's a word that will help you and heal you and get you out from underneath the failures of your past. It's not easy. It's hard because people aren't always fair, and life isn't always fair. But faith says, "I'm trusting God to take care of it." If you will let go of the things that people have done to you, God will bless you beyond your wildest dreams. If you are willing and obedient, you can see miracles take place in your life.

16

OVERCOMING THE GUILT OF MY PAST

The dictionary says that *guilt* is "a state of knowing that you deserve punishment." Guilt is your conscience telling you, "I know I did something wrong, and I know that I should be punished for what I've done."

When we sin, something inside of us lets us know that we deserve to be punished. But when you know that Jesus took your punishment on the cross, you realize you do not have to beat yourself up for the things you've done wrong. However, if guilt is allowed to fester in your life long enough, you'll end up depressed and ashamed, and you'll walk under a spirit of failure. You'll never have the joy God wants you to have until you've dealt with your guilt.

The Bible says the devil is the accuser of the brethren. If you are born again, then he will constantly accuse you of all your failures. His plan is to cause you to be so weighed down with guilt that you will live under a spirit of failure all of your life.

> You see, if the enemy can cause you to walk in guilt and self-condemnation, then he can actually sabotage your earthly destiny and rob you of your heavenly rewards.

You see, if the enemy can cause you to walk in guilt and self-condemnation, then he can actually sabotage your earthly destiny and rob you of your heavenly rewards. Oh, you'll still go to heaven, but you'll lose the rewards you could have earned because the devil messed with your mind and made you feel guilty, guilty for sins that Christ has already forgiven. That's how he can actually steal your future. If he can cause you to feel bad about yourself, about your past, and about your life, then he'll keep you from using your faith. He'll keep you from doing greater things for God and from receiving and enjoying all the promises of God.

Think about it. No matter who we are, we've all done things we wish we hadn't done. We've all had regrets from our past. We all have skeletons in our closet. We've all failed and fallen short of the glory of God.

The devil's job is to accuse people who love the Lord. His job is to accuse the brethren of their failures and to try to hold them down spiritually and emotionally. He doesn't accuse people in the bars who don't love him. He doesn't accuse people in the world. He goes after people who love the Lord. His plan is to make believers like us think we are too much of a failure to make it. He tries to make us think that no one is as bad as we are, and he wants us to doubt our salvation.

Since none of us are perfect, and we've all had failures, his job is pretty easy most of the time. Many of us start to crumble when the devil repeatedly throws our failures in our faces. He loves to continually remind us of the things that we've done wrong.

> *The devil is your spiritual enemy and his strategy is to tempt you with sin, get you to fall into the sin...*

The devil is your spiritual enemy and his strategy is to tempt you with sin, get you to fall into the sin, and then throw that sin in your face for the rest of your life. He will whisper in your ear and say, "Nobody is as bad as you. You're no good. God can't use someone like you. If you were really saved, you wouldn't have done what you did."

As believers we can overcome guilt by confessing our

sin, turning from our sin, and receiving forgiveness. In other words, say, "God, I'm sorry for what I did. I've made up my mind to do everything I can to turn from that sin in my life, and now, God, I claim and receive Your forgiveness in my life." Remember what 1 John 1:9 says: "If we confess our sins, he is faithful and just to forgive us our sins, and to cleanse us from all unrighteousness." We are forgiven for all unrighteousness, not just some, but all.

> The Bible goes on to tell us that we can overcome the guilt of our past. We can overcome the enemy's accusations by the Blood of the Lamb and by the word of our testimony.

The Bible goes on to tell us that we can overcome the guilt of our past. We can overcome the enemy's accusations by the Blood of the Lamb and by the word of our testimony. When you said, "God, please forgive me," He forgave you. When you said, "Lord, I'm a low-down dirty dog, and I don't deserve your forgiveness. But God, please cleanse me now", He forgave you and washed your sins away.

But you can still feel unforgiven, if you let the devil create doubt in your mind. You need to understand the truth about your forgiveness and be able to speak against any doubts that the devil puts in your mind. The words you speak can determine whether or not you can overcome the haunting feelings of past guilt and go on to build an intimate relationship with Jesus Christ.

To understand the importance of applying the Blood of Christ to your life, you must recall the story of Moses and the Passover. When God chose Moses to lead the children of Israel out of slavery in Egypt, He had Moses repeatedly ask Pharaoh to let the Children of Israel go.

On some occasions Pharaoh agreed to let them go, usually after God had sent some miraculous event or terrible plague at Moses' spoken command. But each time Moses agreed to remove the plague, Pharaoh changed his mind and refused to let the Hebrew people go. On the tenth time, however, God achieved the release of His people by sending a death angel to kill all the first-born in the whole region, both man and animal.

In order to spare His people, God had them prepare a sign on all their homes. The death angel would see the sign, and pass over those homes, and not harm any person or animal belonging to that household. This was the origin of the Jewish Passover celebration.

What was the sign? Each family unit of the Hebrew people was to slaughter a lamb and drain its blood into a basin. Then the children of Israel had to get a branch of hyssop, dip it into the blood, and sprinkle the blood of the lamb over the lentil or doorpost of their home. Then they had to apply some of the blood on each side of the door. When the death angel saw the blood, he knew this home was "under the blood," i.e., in a covenant relationship with God. The angel would pass over that home and spare everyone in it. The blood above and on either side of the door was very symbolic, a symbol of the cross where Jesus Christ, the Lamb of God, shed His Blood for the sins of the world. Those who have been born again by accepting Jesus Christ as their personal savior, are "under the Blood," and God's wrath will pass over them without harm.

Here's what you have to do when guilt is destroying you. You must confess the sins that you know you're guilty of, and then you must settle in your heart that the Blood of Jesus is more powerful than your past.

For example, here's what you have to do when guilt is destroying you. You must confess the sins that you know you're guilty of, and then you must settle in your heart that the Blood of Jesus is more powerful than your past. You confess the power that's in the Blood. Then you say out loud, "Yes, I did do what you accused me of, devil, and I was wrong, and I failed God. But because I confess all of my sins, I am cleansed by the Blood of Jesus, and the Blood is more powerful than my past."

In the old covenant, the High Priest would sprinkle the blood on the mercy seat in the holy of holies. When the blood was applied to the mercy seat, the sins of the people were forgiven. All the ceremony and symbolism of the Blood on the doorposts pointed forward to Christ, the Lamb of God, slain from the foundation of the world.

Your own sin will condemn you. But when the Blood of Jesus is applied, your sin can no longer condemn you. Your sin can no longer hold you down. If the enemy

> *Your own sin will condemn you. But when the Blood of Jesus is applied, your sin can no longer condemn you.*

can cause you to live under a feeling of guilt, then he can steal your joy, your peace, and your destiny. If he can make you think that God is mad at you, you won't even bother trying to use your faith. The enemy's plan is to make you think you've gone too far. He wants you to think that God can never forgive you for all that you've done.

Let me tell you how you know you are saved. It's not because you never sin anymore. That person doesn't exist. You know you are saved when you realize you're a sinner who cannot be saved by your own effort, you've laid all your sins at the feet of Jesus Christ, and you've asked Him to forgive you and to be your Lord and Savior.

Generally speaking, when saved people sin, they want to kick themselves for a week in remorse over their behavior. When they sin and fall down, they get back up, trusting God and depending upon Him to do better.

You need to be aware of the difference between guilt and conviction. When you sin and fail God, the Holy Spirit convicts you so you will repent and get it behind you. But guilt may cause you to stay away from God. Conviction draws you to God, and guilt usually causes you to avoid God.

> *You need to be aware of the difference between guilt and conviction.*

Jesus didn't come to judge the world, but to save it (John 3:17). So if you are saved and weighed down with guilt, you have to know it's not God judging you. It's not even God blaming you; it is the devil trying to condemn you. Oh, you may need to confess your sins to God, but if you've done that and you're still weighed down, it's the devil.

When guilt comes into your life, you don't come to church. You tend to avoid church, and you don't seek out godly friends, you stay away from them. But if you love the Lord, and you are on a guilt trip, you need to confess your sins knowing that God's grace is sufficient for you. Repent and get back to church and to your Christian friends. If you'll keep on repenting, He'll keep on forgiving.

"But, Bishop, I did confess my sins, and I still don't feel forgiven." Let me tell you, you cannot go by your feelings. You have to go by what God's Word says. God said you're the righteousness of God. So, when you confess your sins, whether you feel it or whether you don't, you must trust in what God says in the Bible. I don't pay my tithes because I feel like it. I pay my tithes because God said it, and I do it. I don't forgive you because I feel like it; I do it because God commanded me to do so, and I don't say I'm free of guilt because I feel it. I say it because God has said it.

> *There's a certain type of person who continually struggles with guilt. If you are that kind of person, then you will probably have a hard time forgiving others.*

There's a certain type of person who continually struggles with guilt. If you are that kind of person, then you will probably have a hard time forgiving others. That's because the Bible says, if you don't forgive others, God won't forgive you. You must be willing to release others from their load of sin for God to release you. Forgiveness must flow from you if it's to flow to you.

Sin will always leave you feeling guilty. God's laws are

for our protection, and so when you break God's laws, the laws are really breaking you. But the Bible says there is no condemnation for those that are in Christ Jesus (Romans 8:1).

There is no condemning sentence for those who will confess their sins and turn to the Lord.

> The enemy's plan is for you to feel such guilt that you'll say, "Oh, what's the use?"

The enemy's plan is for you to feel such guilt that you'll say, "Oh, what's the use?" Sometimes we wallow in guilt because we feel like such failures. And we beat ourselves up emotionally because of the things we've done wrong. But you need to know that Jesus has already paid the price for all of your sins, He took your punishment, and you don't have to punish yourself anymore. So receive His forgiveness now and get on with your life. Go on with your bad self.

You know the story of how Judas betrayed our Lord for thirty pieces of silver. Then Peter denied he even knew who Jesus was. Judas failed and Peter failed. Two different issues, but they both failed. Peter repented of his sins, and God turned it around. Judas didn't repent, and he ended up killing himself. Both men were guilty of grievous sins and both men felt guilt and condemnation. But only one of them repented and went on with God, the other one's life ended in tragedy. All Judas had to do was confess his sins, receive forgiveness, and overcome the enemy by the Blood of the Lamb and the word of his testimony. If God can forgive you of what you've done wrong, then you can forgive yourself. Judas could have been restored and finished his ministry, if he had only seen his guilt as a warning sign that he could still repent of his sins and be cleansed and forgiven of all his sin and guilt.

You can overcome the guilt of your past no matter who you are or what you have done, if you will simply turn to the Lord and repent of your sins. The grace of God is flowing towards you right now. No sin is too great for the Blood of Jesus to wash away. No sin is beyond His forgiveness if you will simply call on the name of the

> You can overcome the guilt of your past no matter who you are or what you have done, if you will simply turn to the Lord and repent of your sins.

Lord. I am telling you that God Almighty, whose single command can wipe out all of your sin in an instant, is waiting for you to repent.

It was Resurrection Sunday as Mary approached the tomb of Jesus Christ. An angel appeared to her and said, "Go tell the disciples and Peter that Jesus has risen." You see, Peter had failed Christ in such a way, he felt like he could not go on. He felt condemnation in his life. He felt as though he was no good, so God sent an angel to reach out to him and let him know *personally* that God wasn't mad and that everything was going to be all right. God wants me to be your angel, to be a messenger of grace to you. He is telling you, through my words, that all is forgiven, and He's not mad at you, and He's going to work everything out in your life.

> The devil's plan is for you to feel so bad about yourself that you quit God and begin to backslide.

The devil's plan is for you to feel so bad about yourself that you quit God and begin to backslide. His plan is for you to feel so guilty that you quit using your faith in the Lord. The enemy wants you to think it's too hard being a Christian. But the Bible says it's the way of the transgressor that's hard. See, it's hard going to jail. You think it's hard living for the Lord; well, it's hard going through a lengthy prison sentence. You think it's hard living for the Lord; it's also hard being on the run and being afraid of the police following you down the street.

Paul knew a lot about failure. He said, "I am not practicing what I like to do and I'm doing the very thing that I hate. I want to do good, but sometimes the very evil I don't want to do I find myself doing" (Romans 7:15). Paul knew that there was always a struggle in the flesh. He knew that even though one is born again, the flesh would always try to take over.

Maybe you've made a lot of mistakes in the past, and perhaps you've failed God more times than you can count. The good news is you can be forgiven, you can go on, and you can start over. I've let the Lord down more times than I can count, but I keep on repenting, and He keeps on forgiving. If He can use somebody like me, then He can use somebody like you.

"Oh, Bishop, you don't know how many times I've failed. You don't know the things that I've done. I am too unworthy." Welcome to the club! None of us are worthy. We've all failed, and we've all made mistakes! And, yes, we all have skeletons in our closet. Even though you know you are unworthy, you have to understand that the Blood of Jesus makes everything all right.

You see, the Blood of Jesus speaks for you, and it says you are not guilty. It says that you are worthy. It's time to get over the feelings of unworthiness in your life because as long as you feel unworthy, you'll never believe that God wants to help you. And, as long as you feel unworthy, you'll never exercise your faith the way God wants you to. As long as you feel unworthy, you'll never believe God to get a better house. As long as you feel unworthy, you'll never believe God to get a better job, and you'll never believe God to bring you a godly husband or wife.

Paul was a man who knew about guilt. He was a religious zealot who made a lot of mistakes. Before he came to Christ, he thought he was following God, but he was an accomplice to murder. He knew what he was talking about when he said, "I'm forgetting what

As long as you feel unworthy, you'll never believe God to get a better job, and you'll never believe God to bring you a godly husband or wife.

lies behind, and I'm reaching forward to what lies ahead. I will press toward the goal of the prize of the upward call of God in Christ Jesus" (Philippians 3:13-14).

Paul is saying, if you are going to have success in your life, you'll have to get your past behind you. He knew you would have to get your past under the Blood. He knew that even though you feel guilty for what you've done, you still have to open your mouth and confess the power that's in the Blood. He knew that if you are going to overcome the guilt feelings, you have to reach forward to what lies ahead, knowing you're forgiven through the Blood of Jesus.

Even though you feel unworthy, God wants you to know that the Blood of Jesus has covered your past, and everything is going to be all right. You don't have to live under a spirit of failure any longer. God sent me to tell you that He has risen, all has been forgiven, and everything is going to be all right. So snap out of it!

One thing you will learn about God is, He never dwells on past failures. He's a rewarder of faith and that's why He's talking to you about your future right now. It's time to get over your past and just go on with your life. Sometimes you have to let go of some old friends that are pulling you down, so you can focus your mind on God.

> *One thing you will learn about God is, He never dwells on past failures. He's a rewarder of faith.*

We all have a spiritual enemy that wants to keep us from the blessings of God. If he can cause us to disobey God's Word, then he can stop our blessings. If he can get us to hold on to the past, then he can stop our blessings. If he can get us to live in guilt, then he can stop our blessings.

But if we will diligently obey God and are careful to do all He commands us, He will command His blessings on us, and they will overtake us wherever we go. I am not wishing for my luck to change, I am obeying God's Word and He is changing my luck.

There is a time in all of our lives that hand-me-downs

and leftovers are a blessing. But when you know who you are in Christ, you will know that God made you to live in the best house on your block. When you know that you are a royal priesthood, you'll know that the best is none too good for you. It's time to put God first in every part of your life and watch how God blesses you. It's time to obey God in every part of your life, and watch God's blessings overtake you.

About The Author

Bishop Dennis Leonard is the Pastor and Founder of Heritage Christian Center in Denver, Colorado, which is recognized as one of the most successful churches in America. Heritage Christian Center serves over 12,000 people in weekly attendance.

Perhaps Bishop Leonard's greatest achievement has been his ability to attract and retain one of the most ethnically diverse congregations in America. He has accomplished at Heritage Christian Center what many churches from different denominations have found almost impossible to achieve – it has broken down racial, denominational, social and economic barriers and has successfully bridged that gap between these different ethnic groups, forging different cultural and economic interests into one cohesive, loving unit.

Bishop Leonard has been described by his peers, and the greater secular and spiritual community, as a true leader and an example to follow in the Ministry of Reconciliation between races and denominations.

He is a visionary and answers the call of missions both overseas and here in the United States. It is his firm belief that the church must be mobilized almost as if it were an army to do the work of the ministry.

One of Bishop Leonard's most outstanding success stories is the establishment of a widespread prison outreach. The Heritage Christian Center Prison Ministry literally receives countless numbers of letters weekly from incarcerated men and women nationwide. The Prison Ministry Team consistently visits one or more prisons every day throughout the state of Colorado and the neighboring region. In 1997, Bishop Leonard, with the congregation of Heritage Christian Center supporting his vision, purchased and installed satellite dishes in every prison in the state of Colorado in order to meet the desperate need for Christian television within the prison walls.

Bishop Leonard looks for every opportunity possible to preach the Gospel and minister to the lost. As a result of this effort to find avenues for the ministry, he believes that national television is a critical importance to his mission and the mission of Heritage Christian Center.

He currently airs his weekly television program, *'Touching a Hurting World'* on the Black Entertainment Network (BET). This program reaches hundreds of thousands of television households all over the United States in virtually every major city in America, in addition, Bishop Leonard airs two times weekly on the Trinity Broadcasting Network on the Denver, Colorado affiliate.

Bishop Leonard has established a new project at Heritage Christian Center called, "Project Heritage". The mission of Project Heritage is to reach outside the four walls of the church and into the community in order to touch the lives of people where they are hurting. Project Heritage provides housing, job-training, counseling and childcare to families who are trying to rebuild their lives.

And finally, in September 1999, Bishop Leonard was consecrated Bishop of Multi-Cultural Ministries in the Full Gospel Baptist Church Fellowship. Bishop Leonard is the first white man to be consecrated as Bishop with the Full Gospel Baptist Church Fellowship headed by International Presiding Bishop, Bishop Paul S. Morton, Sr.. This new task at hand will open the doors for Bishop Leonard to spread the vision that God gave him several years ago, "It's not a black thing, it's not a white thing, it's a Jesus thing." The multi-cultural ministry that God began and established at Heritage Christian Center can now be taken to the world.

Do You Want To Receive Jesus Christ as Your Lord and Savior?

The Bible says, *"That if thou shalt confess with thy mouth the Lord Jesus, and shalt believe in thine heart that God raised him from the dead, thou shalt be saved. For with the heart man believeth unto righteousness; and with the mouth confession is made unto salvation"* [Romans 10:9,10].

If you want to receive Jesus Christ as the Lord and Savior of your life, sincerely pray the prayer below from your heart;

Jesus, I believe that You died for me and that You rose from the dead. I confess to You that I am a sinner and that I need your forgiveness. Forgive me Lord of my sins and cleanse me from my unrighteousness. Come into my life and give me eternal life. I confess You now as my Lord and my Savior. Begin today to make me the person that I need to be. Put in me those things that need to be in me and remove those things that need to come out. Thank you for dying on the cross for me.
In Jesus' name, Amen!

Signed _____ Date _____

Name _____

Address_____

City _____ State _____ Zip_____

Phone (h)_____

E-mail: _____

Write To Us:
We want to hear from you and we would like to send you information that will help you with your new walk with the Lord.
Dennis Leonard Ministries
9495 East Florida Avenue • Denver, CO 80231 • 303-369-8514
WWW.DENNISLEONARDMINISTRIES.COM

My Personal Notes

My Personal Notes

My Personal Notes

MY PERSONAL NOTES

MY PERSONAL NOTES

My Personal Notes

My Personal Notes

My Personal Notes

My Personal Notes